KU-048-307

CITYSPOTS
EDINBURGH

Zoë Ross

Written by Zoë Ross
Original photography by Robin Gauldie
Front cover photography © David Robertson/Alamy Images
Series design based on an original concept by Studio 183 Limited

Produced by Cambridge Publishing Management Limited
Project Editor: Catherine Burch
Layout: Julie Crane
Maps: PC Graphics
Reproduced by permission of Ordnance Survey on behalf of HMSO. © Crown
Copyright 2006. All rights reserved. Ordnance Survey Licence number 100035725.
Transport map: © Communicarta Ltd

Published by Thomas Cook Publishing
A division of Thomas Cook Tour Operations Limited
Company Registration No. 1450464 England
PO Box 227, Unit 18, Coningsby Road
Peterborough PE3 8SB, United Kingdom
email: books@thomascook.com
www.thomascookpublishing.com
+ 44 (0) 1733 416477
ISBN-13: 978-184157-624-4
ISBN-10: 1-84157-624-7

First edition © 2006 Thomas Cook Publishing
Text © 2006 Thomas Cook Publishing
Maps © 2006 Thomas Cook Publishing
Project Editor: Diane Ashmore
Production/DTP: Steven Collins

Printed and bound in Spain by GraphyCems

CONTENTS

SYMBOLS & ABBREVIATIONS

The following symbols are used throughout this book:

ⓐ address　ⓣ telephone　ⓕ fax　ⓔ email　ⓦ website address
ⓛ opening times　ⓝ public transport connections　ⓘ important

The following symbols are used on the maps:

ⓘ information office	○ city
✈ airport	○ large town
➕ hospital	○ small town
🛡 police station	= motorway
🚌 bus station	— main road
🚆 train station	— minor road
Ⓜ metro	— railway
✝ cathedral	
❶ numbers denote featured cafés & restaurants	

Hotels and restaurants are graded by approximate price as follows:
£ budget　££ mid-range　£££ expensive

▶ *Edinburgh castle dominates the city landscape*

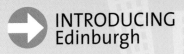

INTRODUCING
Edinburgh

Introduction

Perched on the prehistoric remains of a volcanic landscape and on the edge of the Forth flowing in from the North Sea, Edinburgh, nicknamed the 'Athens of the North', is considered by many to be Britain's most beautiful city.

Divided in two between the medieval Old Town and the 18th-century New Town, the city centre has a split personality. While you can soak up the romantic atmosphere of cobbled streets and tiny alleyways and sense the power of the great Stewart monarchs in and around the Royal Mile, so too can you marvel at the vision and grandeur of the Georgian architects who created such splendid crescents and circuses for the privileged classes beneath the castle's gaze. Even if history isn't your thing, you can't fail to be impressed by the brooding spires, rugged crags and windswept coastline that all form part of Edinburgh's charm.

The Edinburgh Festival and the New Year's Hogmanay are the most popular times to visit, but don't miss the opportunity to come or return at other quieter times of year, when the world-class museums and exhibition centres can be taken in at a more leisurely pace. And don't overlook the superb shopping and dining possibilities. For a city that was once considered rather matronly, designer outlets and haute cuisine have entered Edinburgh's consciousness and have changed her face into a true style destination. Part of this turnaround has been due to the confidence boost Edinburgh received after the return of the Scottish parliament to the city in 1999. For a decade or so prior to that it had clearly been playing second fiddle to its rival Glasgow in the tourist stakes. Meanwhile, the University of Edinburgh, considered one of the best places of learning in Britain, means that the city has a youthful buzz about it for almost 12 months of the year.

It's not all about urban attractions, either. One of the most attractive aspects of Edinburgh life is that within just a few kilometres, you can be outside the city bustle and deep in the heart of rolling countryside, breathing in fresh Scottish air.

The view from the castle ramparts is one of Edinburgh's best

When to go

CLIMATE

Despite its reputation for being the 'chilly north', Edinburgh's climate rarely differs to the south by more than a few degrees in winter. Settled snowfall is usually reserved for the outer city areas and there is far less rain here than in Glasgow to the west. That said, on windy days, the temperature can feel bitter, as the gusts sweep in off the coast, and hats, scarves and gloves are definitely called for. Temperatures between November and March average 3–12°C (37–53°F). Hot summers, however, are also a rarity, although fine, sunny days can add a wonderful glow to the city landscape. Summer temperatures average 15–23°C (59–73°F). Weather in Edinburgh is also changeable by the hour and what can start out a beautiful sunny morning can turn into a damp, grey afternoon and vice versa, so visitors should always be prepared by wearing layers and carrying umbrellas. While winter lacks the warmth, there are plenty of things to attract visitors including the atmospheric Christmas Market on Princes Street Gardens. In contrast, while summer may be a nicer climate in which to explore, crowds of tourists, particularly during the Edinburgh Festival, can make the streets a challenge to navigate.

COSTS

British rail fares remain disproportionately expensive compared to the rest of the world, but the rise of low-cost airlines such as easyJet and Scotland's own flyglobespan, means visiting Edinburgh for a short break is a very viable option.

Costs of accommodation escalate beyond all recognition during the Festival season (see pages 14–15), and that's if you can get a room – these are normally booked at least a year in advance. The rest of the year, however, particularly autumn and winter, there are many good deals in all but the top-class hotels.

ANNUAL EVENTS

Edinburgh has a jam-packed calendar of annual events, as well as events that might be specific to a certain year. Carnivals, markets, sporting fixtures and street fairs all combine to make this one of the most party-happy cities in Britain. Listings magazines such as *The List* highlight any particular activities for that week of publication, and the tourist office will also have details of current and up-and-coming activities.

January

In late January **Burns Night** is celebrated throughout Edinburgh to honour the great Scottish poet Robbie Burns. A custom for over 200 years, the meal begins with the Selkirk Grace. The company is asked to stand, and clap slowly while a piper leads the chef, carrying the haggis, to the top table. The most senior guest then recites Burns' famous poem 'to a Haggis'. After the meal there are various speeches, including the Immortal Memory speech dedicated to Burns' work and a Toast to the Lassies, ending with a rendition of 'Auld Lang Syne' (25 Jan).

April

Ceilidh Culture is an annual celebration of traditional Scottish songs, music, dance and storytelling held in various locations throughout the city (early April).
ⓦ www.ceilidhculture.co.uk

June

Pride Scotland is Edinburgh's version of Gay Pride. There are events all around the city but the main venue is Preston Park (mid-June). The national agricultural show, the **Royal Highland Show**, has been drawing crowds in June for many years. Showjumping events, sheep shearing and livestock displays are all part of the fun (late June).

July

The **Jazz and Blues Festival** is a city-wide party of syncopated beats, including Mardi Gras (Grassmarket) and Jazz on a Summer's Day, an open-air series of concerts in Princes Street Gardens (late July/early Aug).

August

The **Edinburgh Fringe Festival** and **International Festival** take over the capital (see pages 14–15).

Since 1950 the **Edinburgh Military Tattoo** has also been a highlight of the city's calendar, full of pageantry and pomp, held in front of the floodlit castle. The event is so popular that it is broadcast on television all over the world and more than 200,000 people attend the three-week event. The Tattoo starts with Scottish regimental bands emerging carrying effigies of William Wallace and Robert the Bruce and playing traditional Scottish songs that reflect the country's past. Despite the celebration of Scotland, the Tattoo has also become an international event, with regiments from other countries invited to attend, and the performing acts are global in flavour too, with past participants hailing from as far afield as Fiji and Nepal. The finale is a rousing rendition of the Evening Hymn, the sounding of the Last Post,

and the Lone Piper, before a spectacular fireworks display.
Tickets are hard to come by but go on sale in August for the
following year's Festival.

ⓐ Tattoo Ticket Sales Office, 32–34 Market Street ① 0131 225 8627
ⓦ www.edinburgh-tattoo.co.uk

Edinburgh International Book Festival in Charlotte Square
Gardens brings writers from all over the world to discuss their work.
There's also live music, family activities and open-air bars and cafés
(mid-Aug).

Edinburgh International Film Festival screens new releases,
independent and arthouse movies, and presents talks and
retrospectives of actors and directors (late Aug).

ⓦ www.edfilmfest.co.uk

September

Edinburgh Mela is Scotland's multicultural celebration in Pilrig Park,
with a strong emphasis on Asia. Expect bands, dances, Bollywood
spectacles and much more (early Sept).

ⓦ www.edinburgh-mela.co.uk

November

Like the rest of Britain, Edinburgh celebrates the failing of the
Gunpowder Plot to blow up the Houses of Parliament in 1605 by
building an effigy of the chief traitor Guy Fawkes and holding
fireworks displays. There are many displays around the city on
Bonfire Night, but the main event is at Meadowbank Stadium (5 Nov).

December

The **Edinburgh Christmas Festival** has a traditional German
market selling toys and trinkets, as well as live entertainment

and a giant Ferris wheel, the Edinburgh Eye, on Princes Street
Gardens.

One of the liveliest events in the Edinburgh calendar are the
New Year's Eve celebrations known as **Hogmanay** on 31 December.
Vast crowds of up to 100,000 people join the street party to watch
fireworks, live bands, which usually have Scottish roots such as
Texas and The Proclaimers, and see in the new year. On 29 December
there is a torchlight procession, on 30 December, known as The
Night Afore, street performers hit the streets, and on New Year's Day
the One O'Clock Run race takes place down the Royal Mile.

PUBLIC HOLIDAYS
New Year's Day/Hogmanay 1 & 2 January
Good Friday, Easter Sunday & Easter Monday Late March or
early April
Spring Holiday Mid-April Monday
May Day First Monday in May
Victoria Day Last Monday in May
Summer Bank Holiday Last Monday in August
Autumn Bank Holiday Monday in mid-September
Christmas Day 25 December
Boxing Day 26 December
(If Christmas Day, Boxing Day or New Year's Day falls on a
Saturday or Sunday, the next weekday becomes a public
holiday.)

▶ *Thousands celebrate Hogmanay in Edinburgh*

The Edinburgh Festival & Fringe

For the month of August Edinburgh becomes unrecognisable from its normally sedate image, when the capital is overrun with actors, street buskers, musicians, dancers and a whole load of tourists who flock here to perform or watch a vast array of dramatic offerings.

⬤ *Festival-goers fill the streets of Edinburgh*

Both the International Festival and the Fringe began in 1947. The International Festival is a professional performing arts festival offering a packed programme of theatre, dance and music in all the city's main theatres and many other venues too. Well-established theatre companies from all over the world come here to offer the capital their talents.

The Fringe was begun as a cultural postwar initiative to encourage those outside the mainstream of the performing arts to stage their own shows, and this continues to this day – anyone can perform at the Fringe as long as they book their venue well enough in advance. Today performers come from all over the globe, aiming to achieve press attention and rave reviews for their work, and to be a part of the largest arts festival in the world. Over recent years more than 700 groups or individuals have performed here each year. One of the most popular parts of the Fringe is the comedy element, with stand-up comedians all vying for the prestigious Perrier Award, which has launched the career of many in the past. Away from the indoor venues, the streets of the city are also full of celebratory verve. This is particularly true of the Royal Mile, which is crammed with buskers, mime artists and portrait painters for the month of the Festival.

The Festivals can be quite overwhelming. There's so much to see and do that it can be hard to choose, pushy punters thrusting flyers into your face can get irritating and the crowds make getting to venues and securing tickets quite a challenge. Each year a Festival programme is published, detailing what's on and where, and it pays to study it and decide what is of interest beforehand, not least because for the most popular events tickets sell out very fast indeed.

Fringe Box Office ☎ (0131) 226 5138 🌐 www.edinburgh-festivals.com

History

Edinburgh's hills – Arthur's Seat, Blackford Hill, Craiglockhart Hill and Castle Rock itself – are natural fortresses that attracted settlers as early as the first millennium BC. Castle Rock may even have been occupied for many centuries before the Roman invasion of Caledonia in AD 80–84. The Romans, however, bypassed Castle Rock but built a fort at Cramond, on the Firth of Forth.

In the 6th century AD, Castle Rock was a stronghold of the Christian British kingdom of the Gododdin, who called it Dun Eideann (Eideann's Fort), a name which became Edinburgh or 'Edwin's Fortress', after the Anglo-Saxon conquest of southeast Scotland in the 7th century AD. The Angles were eventually ousted by Malcolm II, King of Scots, in 1018 and Edinburgh and its castle soon grew in size and importance. In 1128, King David II founded Holyrood Abbey, at the foot of the Royal Mile. Over the following centuries Edinburgh grew to occupy the hillsides between Holyrood and the castle – the district now known as the Old Town.

Too close to the border for comfort, Edinburgh was frequently sacked and occupied by the English, and the city did not become Scotland's capital until 1436, when King James II (1430–60) made it his royal seat. Previous Scots kings had ruled from Dunfermline in Fife or Dumbarton on the Clyde, but Edinburgh was to be the home of the Scottish Crown and the Stewart dynasty for almost three centuries.

The Stewarts were unlucky monarchs – James II was killed when he was blown up by one of his own cannons, James III was assassinated by discontented nobles, James IV died in battle against the English at Flodden in 1513, James V died of despair after yet another defeat at English hands at Solway Moss, and his daughter

Mary was executed by her cousin, Queen Elizabeth I of England. With the Union of the English and Scottish Crowns in 1603 her son, James VI of Scotland, became James I of England, ushering in a more peaceful era, although Edinburgh continued to change hands between Scottish, Royalist and Parliamentarian forces during the civil wars of the mid-17th century, when Scotland sided with King Charles I – another unlucky Stewart, beheaded in 1649.

The Act of Union of 1707, uniting Scotland with England, ended Edinburgh's glory days as Scotland's capital, although Charles Edward Stewart (better known as Bonnie Prince Charlie) briefly made it his base in 1745, after defeating a Hanoverian army at Prestonpans. In other ways, however, the 18th century was a golden age for Edinburgh, which became a centre for philosophy, science and the arts, while the gracious Georgian streets of the New Town became the sought-after address for the wealthy and influential.

With the Industrial Revolution, Edinburgh spread to include the seaport of Leith and new suburbs such as Portobello, while railways connected it with London and the rest of Britain. But the loss of political power to London and economic pre-eminence to Glasgow, Scotland's new industrial powerhouse, undermined some of Edinburgh's self-confidence.

The birth of the Edinburgh International Festival in 1947 was the start of a deliberate campaign to restore the city's fortunes, which culminated half a century later with devolution and the return of a Scottish parliament to Edinburgh after 290 years of rule from London. Edinburgh entered the 21st century as the true capital of Scotland once again.

Lifestyle

The citizens of Edinburgh are generally considered to be rather reserved and taciturn, particularly in comparison to their more gregarious neighbours in Glasgow, although anyone who has experienced the unfriendly anonymity of many capital cities would find this quite absurd. In reality, hop into any taxi or queue up at any shop counter and you'll find the locals like nothing better than to pass the time of day, usually with some reference to the weather.

. And it is the weather that largely shapes the capital's character. From wet to sunny to wet again in a matter of hours, the changeability means that although Edinburghers love to snuggle in warm pubs and exchange gossip over a pint of beer, they rarely miss an opportunity to get to the great outdoors when a hint of sunshine comes through.

Edinburgh may be a capital, but it's a small one. While property prices are slowly creeping up to meet the excesses of the south of Britain, many locals are still able to afford to live in or very near the city centre. This makes for a communal, convivial atmosphere where work and home live side by side. There's also little of the age divide that dominates many city landscapes. While there are bars and clubs that are exclusively the preserve of the young, you're far more likely to see trendy university students sitting happily beside septuagenarians in the city's multitude of old-style pubs.

The face of the city changes entirely in August, however, when the world and his wife descend on Edinburgh for the annual arts festival. While locals are justifiably proud of the event, many see it as an opportunity to get away, not least for the extortionately high prices that they can charge for renting out their flats or homes at a time when accommodation is at a premium.

◆ *Enjoying a quiet pint in a New Town pub*

Clearly August is prime tourist season, but don't expect a cultural wasteland the rest of the time. Visitors flock here all the year round, and you'll hear as many accents from the rest of Britain and the world as you will the traditional Scottish brogue from people who have chosen to make this beautiful city their home.

Culture

Edinburgh is, without doubt, one of Britain's cultural hot spots with festivals, theatrical events, music and dance going on all year round. The information given here is a general overview of what you might expect, but to find out more about what is going on at the time of your visit head to the tourist office on Princes Street or any newsagent to pick up a copy of the city's listings magazine *The List* or visit the website ⓦ www.edinburgh.org

PERFORMANCE ARTS

Edinburgh's theatrical highlight is undoubtedly the Festival (see pages 14–15) but the rest of the year is also a hotbed of theatrical activity, presenting both Scottish-based events as well as national and international touring companies. While most of the national companies, including Scottish Ballet, Opera and Orchestra, are based in Glasgow, they regularly come to Edinburgh to stage performances. **The Usher Hall** (ⓦ www.usherhall.co.uk) on Lothian Road is the main venue in the city for classical music, jazz and pop concerts, and is also responsible for the programme of events at the Ross Open Air Theatre, which sits beneath the castle in Princes Street Gardens. But it is theatre that is the mainstay of Edinburgh's performing prowess, as can be evidenced by the venues opposite.

● *Edinburgh Playhouse*

Edinburgh Playhouse The city's main theatre, at the top of Leith Walk, is the main venue for touring high-glitz West End productions, predominantly musicals such as *Mamma Mia!* and *My Fair Lady*.
ⓐ 18–22 Greenside Place ⓣ (0870) 606 3424

Festival Theatre There's a year-round programme of drama, opera and ballet at this modern theatre in the Old Town.
ⓐ 13–29 Nicolson Street ⓣ (0131) 529 6000 ⓦ www.eft.co.uk

King's Theatre In the city's West End district, this small theatre stages touring repertory companies, including pantomime at Christmas.
ⓐ 2 Leven Street ⓣ (0131) 529 6000 ⓦ www.eft.co.uk

Royal Lyceum Theatre Edinburgh's own repertory theatre presents a variety of drama genres, with a strong emphasis on Scottish playwrights.
ⓐ Grindlay Street ⓣ (0131) 248 4848 ⓦ www.lyceum.org.uk

Traverse Theatre Established in 1963, the Traverse is one of the city's best-known theatres because of its emphasis on new writing, both from Scotland and abroad.
ⓐ 10 Cambridge Street ⓣ (0131) 228 1404 ⓦ www.traverse.co.uk

VISUAL ARTS

Most of Edinburgh's art galleries are in the New Town and Dean Village (see page 87) and present the finest collection of art in Scotland, ranging from the traditional to the modern conceptual genres. In addition to viewing art, there are many opportunities to buy, from the small and eclectic galleries in the Stockbridge area, to fine art galleries on Dundas Street in the New Town, to the annual Edinburgh Art Fair that takes place each November at the Corn Exchange on Newmarket Road.

MUSEUMS

It could be said that much of Edinburgh itself is a museum, particularly the Old Town where visitors live and breathe its history and which is now a World Heritage Site. The city's finest museum, truly world class in style and content, is the Museum of Scotland (see pages 76–77) detailing everything about the city's national heritage from prehistoric times to the present day, all beautifully and imaginatively laid out and explained. But there are also more quirky attractions such as The Real Mary King's Close (see pages 50–51) and Gladstone's Land on Lawnmarket, which explore how Edinburghers lived in tenement conditions for centuries, offering more of a living history atmosphere. The castle, of course, has unique exhibitions, with the Scottish crown jewels as its highlight. Nature is the theme of two excellent 'museums': Our Dynamic Earth (see page 70) explores all manner of geological and ecological issues to do with the planet, while outside the city centre is the award-winning Scottish Seabird Centre (see page 123) which examines the area's natural avian world.

LITERARY HERITAGE

Three great Scottish writers – Robert Burns, Robert Louis Stevenson and Sir Walter Scott – are celebrated at the Writers' Museum (see pages 77–8) but Edinburgh is a hotbed of literary references, from Ian Rankin's Rebus stories, to Muriel Spark's Jean Brodie, and the working class Leith of Irvine Welsh's *Trainspotting*. There are many literary tours in the city taking visitors past places such as the site of the café where JK Rowling wrote Harry Potter (now a Chinese restaurant) as well as pub crawls with literary associations (ⓦ www.edinburghliterarypubtour.co.uk).

● *George Street is the city's best shopping thoroughfare*

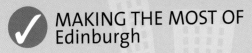

MAKING THE MOST OF
Edinburgh

Shopping

Edinburgh is something of a shopper's paradise, whether you're after designer names in fashion or textiles, one-off pieces from the many quirky boutiques, or simply classic Scottish souvenirs such as tartan, cashmere or whisky.

SHOPPING AREAS

The Royal Mile (see pages 71–3) is the place to head for if you're after traditional Scottish goods, although beware the overly touristy shops, particularly those closest to the castle. Along this stretch of the Old Town you'll find innumerable shops selling all manner of tartan, luxurious cashmere sweaters, and traditional edibles such as shortbread and fudge, in tartan patterned tins. This is also a good place to find Celtic-styled jewellery and, for children, plastic swords and helmets as a nod to the country's warrior past.

Just off the Royal Mile is Cockburn Street, which is well known for its slightly hippie atmosphere, with second-hand clothes, books and record stores, as well as tattoo parlours and everything of an alternative nature.

For upmarket designer names, you can't do better than St Andrew Square and Multrees Walk in the heart of the New Town, where you'll find the luxury of Harvey Nichols and an elegant pedestrianised street flaunting such icons as Louis Vuitton. Just along from here is George Street where slightly cheaper but equally stylish names can be found, such as Jigsaw and Whistles. One-off stylish boutiques are a speciality of the lovely Thistle Street, also in the New Town. The classic

● *Jenners, the* grande dame *of Edinburgh's department stores*

Edinburgh department store is Jenners, which has a slightly old-fashioned feel to it in comparison with its glossy neighbour Harvey Nichols, but is still the shop of choice for most well-to-do Edinburgh ladies.

Princes Street is the most famous shopping street in Edinburgh, but without just cause in terms of retail value. It's little more than a mile-long cluster of everyday high-street stores such as Dixons and British Home Stores. Come for the view, but in terms of shopping you won't find anything here that you couldn't find at home.

The antiques areas of the city are the Grassmarket and West Bow areas in the Old Town and Dundas Street in the New Town, as well as along The Causeway in southern Edinburgh. If you're looking for a piece of art to take home, Stockbridge is the area with the most attractive small galleries.

The main market in Edinburgh is the Farmers' Market (see page 79) each Saturday near the castle.

MALLS

Given Edinburgh's unreliable weather, the city does have its fair share of covered shopping malls, although few offer anything to write home about.

The most central of these are the St James's Centre and the Princes Street Mall, both of which are rather dull in nature, and the latter being an almost no-go, filled as it is with the worst of tourist tat. The St James's, however, does boast a branch of John Lewis, which always has a high reputation for providing everything a department store should, at reasonable prices.

In Leith the Ocean Terminal (see page 107) is attempting to follow the lead of the area's successful regeneration, boasting a

Marks & Spencer food emporium, Debenhams department store and fashion names such as French Connection and Fat Face. It's still, however, a little soulless, and not worth the trip to this area of town simply for shopping purposes.

The largest shopping mall is on the outskirts of the city. Fort Kinnaird Retail Shopping Park (Newcraighall Road) covers 54,000 sq m (584,000 sq ft) and includes major names such as PC World, Laura Ashley, Argos, Mothercare and Next, as well as numerous cafés and fast-food outlets.

Opening Hours

Shops are usually open seven days a week, from 9am to 6pm, although many have shorter hours on Sundays and open late on Thursdays.

LOCAL CRAFTS

Within Edinburgh itself the Tartan Weaving Mill (see page 51) and Scotch Whisky Heritage Centre (see page 51) are the best places to go for these two specialities.

Outside Edinburgh are two further crafts centres well worth a visit. **The Edinburgh Crystal Visitor Centre** in Penicuik (☏ (01968) 675 128) allows visitors to see the glassblowers at work as well as to buy delicate pieces of Edinburgh crystal. The **Glenkinchie Distillery** (ⓦ www.malts.com), 24 km (15 miles) from the city, also offers the opportunity to learn about the distillation of malt whiskies and buy samples to take home.

Eating & drinking

Despite Scotland's reputation for serving everything fried (which isn't entirely unfounded), Edinburgh has a range of top-class restaurants, fashionable cafés and bars, as well as a wide range of budget options. Pub culture is, of course, alive and well and the advantage here is that traditional has not often given way to soulless modern design. Many of the pubs remain as they have been for the past 100 years in both style and atmosphere. For those who prefer a more funky feel, however, there are glitzy bars here too, particularly in areas such as George Street in the New Town.

As would be expected, many of the restaurants and cafés in the Old Town, particularly along the Royal Mile, are either tourist traps or uninteresting chains such as Garfunkel's and Pizza Hut but a few gems can be found away from the main streets. The New Town, however, is the heart of fine dining in the city, while Leith, unsurprisingly, has a string of highly lauded fish and seafood restaurants with the added advantage of sea views.

Scottish restaurants focus heavily on meat and fish, although vegetarians should always be able to find a suitable option, and there are at least two highly respected vegetarian establishments

RESTAURANT CATEGORIES

The following price guide used throughout the book indicates the average price per head for a 2–3 course à la carte dinner, excluding drinks. Lunch will usually be a little cheaper and many restaurants also offer fixed price menus.

£ under £20; ££ £20–30; £££ over £30

🔻 *Traditional meets international in the fast-food stakes*

in the city – the David Bann Restaurant (see page 81) and Henderson's Salad Table (see page 96). In addition there are plenty of ethnic restaurants around the city, including Chinese and Indian, which always offer plenty of vegetarian choices.

There's no hard or fast rule as to whether restaurants include service charges on their bill or not – some do and some don't – so check your bill when paying. If service is not included, it's customary to leave a tip of 10–15 per cent of the cost of the meal. Tips aren't required in pubs if you're only drinking.

Since 26 March 2006 all public places, including restaurants, pubs and bars, have become strictly non-smoking.

MARKETS & PICNICS

The Saturday farmers' market by the castle (see page 79) is a great place to pick up Scottish specialities and if you're lucky enough to have a sunny day, it's ideal for picnic foods. The food hall of Harvey Nichols is a more luxurious option, while the city is scattered with tasty delis such as Relish (Commercial Street, Leith) and speciality shops such as Mellis (Kerr Road, Stockbridge) where you can pick up a selection of tasty Scottish cheeses.

SPECIALITIES

Haggis is probably the most famous Scottish dish, although its description may not appeal to all tastes. Similar to a ball-shaped sausage, it consists of sheep's intestines, heart and liver, minced with onion, oatmeal and various spices, contained within the animal's stomach lining, then boiled and traditionally served with neeps and tatties (mashed swede and potato). If the real thing doesn't appeal, vegetarian haggis made with pulses, vegetables and nuts is increasingly available, although most Scots find the notion an aberration.

Meat plays an important part in Scottish cuisine and you'll see plenty of Aberdeen Angus beef, venison and lamb on restaurant menus, and game such as pheasant and partridge in season. Given its coastal location, fish and seafood are also abundant, and oyster lovers will never go wanting. Cullen Skink is a delicious haddock and potato soup that is very heartening on a cold winter's day, while

Arbroath Smokies are smoked haddocks that originate from the coastal town about 100 miles north of the capital. And, of course, fish and chips of high quality are available all over the city.

For a savoury snack many bakers sell Bridies, which are a take on the Cornish pasty but made with plain instead of puff pastry, and filled with minced beef and onions. Another savoury snack are oatcakes, delicious when served with Scottish cheeses. For a sweet tea-time snack you can't go wrong with traditional Scottish shortbread.

Whisky is the most famous Scottish drink, both malt and blended, made in distilleries around the country. Edinburgh also has its own brewery, the Caledonian, which produces popular ales such as 80 Shilling, named after the original cost of the barrel. Scotland's home-produced soft drink is Irn Bru, a bright orange fizzy concoction that people tend to either love or hate.

◆ A traditional Scottish pub in Leith

Entertainment & nightlife

Edinburgh takes entertainment and nightlife very seriously indeed, although the emphasis tends towards cultural good times rather than bare-faced hedonism. Jazz clubs thrive here and night clubs have a sophisticated edge to them, although anyone looking for a more grungy atmosphere will find plenty of options in the Old Town and West End areas. Tickets for most venues are available at the door.

⬤ *There are 12 screens to choose from in the Omni Centre*

LISTINGS & WHAT'S ON

Edinburgh's main listings magazine (which also covers Glasgow) is the weekly *The List*, available from the tourist office and most newsagents. As well as articles about events relevant to both cities, it gives full listings of club nights, cinemas, theatre, gay events and comedy. It also has an online source, ⓦ www.list.co.uk

CINEMA

As the location for many top-rated films, such as *The Prime of Miss Jean Brodie* and *Trainspotting*, as well as birthplace of Hollywood legend Sean Connery, it's not surprising that Edinburgh is a film-loving city. It has its fair share of cinema chains, the same as any other British city but also has a handful of specialist film venues.

The Cameo Edinburgh's arthouse film venue is set in an historic turn-of-the-century building. There's also a bar and drinks can be taken into the screening area. ❷ 38 Home Street ❶ (0131) 228 4141

The Filmhouse This regional cinema is home to the annual Edinburgh Film Festival (see page 11) and the rest of the year screens popular general releases (but not blockbusters), as well as arthouse films and documentaries. ❷ 88 Lothian Road ❶ (0131) 228 2688

The **Vue** chain of multiplex cinemas has two branches in Edinburgh. In the Omni Centre, at the top of Leith Walk, there is a 12-screen cinema complex showing all the latest releases, while the Ocean Terminal complex in Leith (see page 107) is another multiplex offering. ❷ Omni Centre: Greenside Place ❶ (0131) 556 3523

🔵 *Usher Hall is a popular live music venue*

STAND-UP COMEDY

Edinburgh Festival's Perrier Award, whose past winners have included Frank Skinner and Al Murray, put stand-up comedy firmly on the British map, and the city still has a fondness for the genre throughout the year.

Jongleurs This national comedy club chain opened in the Omni Centre in 2003 and presents popular stand-up comedy every Friday and Saturday night. ③ Greenside Place ☎ (0870) 0111965 ⓦ www.jongleurs.com

The Stand Comedy Club One of the best-known comedy clubs in Britain has high-quality performances seven nights a week. Monday

night is Red Raw beginners' night. Food and drinks also served.
ⓐ 5 York Place ⓣ (0131) 558 7272 ⓦ www.thestand.co.uk

LIVE MUSIC

The city's annual Jazz and Blues Festival (see page 10) draws big names from around the world, but many jazz clubs around the city are full to the rafters with cool cats listening to dulcet tones throughout the year. Recently Jools Holland has had a great success with his Jam House (see page 99) in the New Town and the Scottish National Jazz Orchestra is also based here. For a purely Scottish feel, however, don't miss the many folk music events, a great deal of which are impromptu musical get-togethers in bars such as Sandy Bell's and the Royal Oak (see page 82). Local well-known bands such as The Proclaimers and Shoogelnifty regularly play their home town and shouldn't be missed if one of their gigs coincides with your visit. If you want to dance as well as listen, the Assembly Rooms hold regular ceilidhs, the traditional Scottish folk dancing evenings.
ⓐ Assembly Rooms: 54 George Street ⓣ (0131) 228 1155
ⓦ www.assemblyroomsedinburgh.co.uk

CLUBS & BARS

While not so much of a clubbing city as its western neighbour Glasgow, Edinburgh nevertheless has a thriving scene, both straight and gay, and attracts many big name DJs from the rest of the country. One of the main clubbing areas is Cowgate, which can become rowdy and unpleasant in the early hours of Saturday and Sunday. Traditionally Rose Street has been the main pub crawling area of the city, although George Street, running parallel behind it, has smarter options. The main gay area is at the top of Leith Walk where bars such as CC Blooms and Planet Out are the mainstays.

Sport & relaxation

SPECTATOR SPORTS

Football is the main spectator sport in Edinburgh, with strong competition between Edinburgh's two major clubs, Hearts (Heart of Midlothian) and Hibs (Hibernian). Hearts' home ground is **Tynecastle** on Gorgie Road, and match tickets can be obtained from Ⓦ www.seatbooker.net/hearts, while Hibernian play at the **Easter Road Stadium** with tickets available by telephoning Ⓣ (0131) 661 1875. There's a long-standing rivalry between the two clubs, much of it historical and sectarian, with Hearts traditionally Protestant and Hibs Catholic, but it's largely harmless.

Horseracing is popular. There are 26 race meetings, both flat racing and jump racing, as well as speciality events such as Mardi Gras, at the **Musselburgh Racecourse** along the coast from the city centre. Tickets can be booked on the course's website. Ⓐ Linkfield Road, Musselburgh Ⓣ (0131) 665 2859 Ⓦ www.musselburgh-racecourse.co.uk

Edinburgh has several rugby teams, including the professional Edinburgh Gunners. Rugby Union games are played at weekends at the historic **Murrayfield Stadium** to the west of the city off Roseburn Street. Tickets are elusive but telephone Ⓣ (0131) 346 5000 for more information.

PARTICIPANT SPORTS & RELAXATION
Golf

Golf was invented in nearby St Andrews so it's not surprising that the sport has taken a grip of Edinburgh too. There are six courses near the centre, the most central being the nine-hole Portobello course. The most challenging, however, is the par 71 course at Braid Hills.

Portobello Golf Course ⓐ Stanley Street EH15 1JJ ⓣ (0131) 669 4361
Braid Hills Golf Course ⓐ Braid Hills Approach Road EH10 6JZ
ⓣ (0131) 447 6666

Sailing

There are plenty of opportunities for messing about on the water
in and around Edinburgh, including kayaking, dinghy sailing and
power boating. The company Edinburgh Leisure will organise a
variety of trips and courses.

Edinburgh Leisure ⓐ 54 Nicolson Street ⓣ (0131) 650 1001
ⓦ www.edinburghleisure.co.uk

Skiing

For skiing, Midlothian Snowsports Centre at Hill End is the nearest
skiing opportunity to the city, only 4 km (2 miles) away, and the
slope can be seen from various parts of Edinburgh. But it's only dry
skiing, even if it is the longest dry slope in Britain. For the nearest
snow skiing head for Glenshee, about 100 km (62 miles) north of
Edinburgh near Braemar.

Midlothian Snowsports Centre ⓐ Biggar Road, EH10 7DU
ⓣ (0131) 445 4433 ⓒ 9.30–21.00 Mon–Sat, 9.30–19.00 Sun
Glenshee Ski Centre ⓦ www.ski-glenshee.co.uk

Walking & hiking

For a gentle hill walk within the city itself explore the mound of
Arthur's Seat (see page 73), with its well-maintained footpaths.
Further afield, **Walk Scotland** (ⓦ www.walkscotland.com) organises
a 19 km (12 mile) hike in the Pentland Hills (see page 142), one of
Scotland's regional parks, with great opportunities for birdwatching
and wonderful views.

Accommodation

Like most British cities Edinburgh has accommodation to suit
all budgets, from the ultra luxurious, like the world-famous
The Balmoral, to basic lodgings and motels, to quaint B&Bs both in
and outside the city. Some hotels include breakfast in the room
rate and some don't, so check before you book. In the larger hotels
breakfast is likely to be a full Scottish breakfast, including black
pudding and haggis.

Out of season it's not always necessary to book in advance, but it
is quite straightforward to find hotels on the web or from the
tourist office.

PRICE RATINGS
The following ratings indicate average price per double room
per night – some rooms may be more or less expensive than
the rating suggests, depending on high or low season.
£ under £60; ££ £60–150; £££ over £150

BUDGET HOTELS

Botanic House Hotel £ With views over the nearby Botanic Gardens,
these six en suite rooms offer an elegance and style that you rarely
see at this price. There's also a bar and a beer garden. @ 27 Inverleith
Row ① (0131) 552 2563 ⓦ www.botanichousehotel.com

Davenport House £ A traditionally decorated guest house in a
converted Georgian building, offering a far more luxurious feel than
the price tag would suggest. @ 58 Great King Street ① (0131) 558
8495 ⓦ www.davenport-house.com

Ibis Edinburgh Centre £ Another great location for a great price, just off the Royal Mile and with car parking, which is an added bonus. ⓐ 6 Hunter Square ⓣ (0131) 240 7000 ⓦ www.ibishotel.com

Six Mary's Place £ In the arty atmosphere of Stockbridge this is a lovely converted house decorated in muted pastel shades while retaining original Georgian details. Great value. ⓐ Raeburn Place ⓣ (0131) 332 8965 ⓦ www.sixmarysplace.co.uk

Travelodge Edinburgh Central £ Don't expect any frills here – all you will get is an en suite room and a small selection of snacks in the reception, but for its location in the heart of the Old Town, and price, it can't be beaten. ⓐ 12 St Mary's Street ⓣ (0870) 191 1637 ⓦ www.travelodge.co.uk

MID-RANGE HOTELS

The Bonham ££ Affordable luxury at one of Edinburgh's most popular hotels. All rooms are individually decorated in contemporary style. ⓐ 35 Drumsheugh Gardens ⓣ (0131) 274 7400 ⓦ www.thebonham.com

Malmaison ££ The landmark Leith hotel overlooking the waterfront and set in a former Victorian seamen's mission. Inside everything is minimally designed with bold shapes in muted tones. ⓐ 1 Tower Place ⓣ (0131) 468 5000 ⓦ www.malmaison.com

Mount Royal Ramada Jarvis ££ A good mid-range option for its central location, although its chain hotel atmosphere is a little bland. ⓐ 53 Princes Street ⓣ (0131) 225 7161 ⓦ www.ramadajarvis.co.uk

The Point Hotel ££ One of the finest design hotels in the world – or so its promotion claims. A feel of Manhattan about it, with fluorescent coloured lighting, black and white rooms and wonderful castle views. ⓐ 34 Bread Street ⓣ (0131) 221 5555 ⓦ www.point-hotel.co.uk

Radisson SAS Hotel Edinburgh ££ An excellent location on the Royal Mile and also benefiting from a car park (for a small fee). The health spa, including pool and sauna, is ideal for soothing cobble-tired feet. ⓐ 80 High Street ⓣ (0131) 557 9797 ⓦ www.radissonsas.com

Rick's ££ A lovely boutique hotel with only 10 en suite rooms. The minimalist rooms include angora blankets, soft towelling robes and DVD players. ⓐ 55a Frederick Street ⓣ (0131) 622 7800 ⓦ www.ricksedinburgh.co.uk

LUXURY HOTELS

The Balmoral £££ Part of the Rocco Forte chain, this is the place to stay if money is no object. All the en suite rooms are styled to perfection while the restaurant has earned itself a Michelin star (see page 98). There's also a pool and health club. ⓐ 1 Princes Street ⓣ (0131) 556 2414 ⓦ www.thebalmoralhotel.com

The Caledonian Hilton £££ An Edinburgh institution with 250 rooms, many with castle views, a health club and central location on the corner of Princes Street. ⓐ Princes Street ⓣ (0131) 222 8888 ⓦ www.hilton.co.uk/caledonian

◗ *Malmaison in Leith overlooks the waterfront*

The Carlton £££ Convenient for the Royal Mile and the castle, The Carlton is a famous Edinburgh institution although it is slightly lacking in the personal touch. ⓐ North Bridge ⓣ (0131) 472 3000 ⓦ www.paramount-hotels.co.uk/carlton

Dalhousie Castle £££ About half an hour's drive from the city centre, staying in this converted 13th-century castle is worth it for a special occasion. The cellar restaurant is superb, serving the finest Scottish food. ⓐ Bonnyrigg ⓣ (01875) 820153 ⓦ www.dalhousiecastle.co.uk

The George £££ Set in a listed building and ornately decorated with chandeliers, velvet drapes and original tiles, many of the rooms here have views of the castle. Possibly the finest hotel in town. ⓐ 19–21 George Street ⓣ (0131) 225 1251 ⓦ www.principal-hotels.com

Number Ten Hotel £££ In a beautiful Georgian building in the New Town the Number Ten combines classic charm with modern style. ⓐ 10 Gloucester Place ⓣ (0131) 225 2720 ⓦ www.numbertenhotel.com

The Scotsman £££ Housed in the impressive former *Scotsman* newspaper building, this is an elegant option that also benefits from its own high-tech spa and excellent restaurant. ⓐ North Bridge ⓣ (0131) 556 5565 ⓦ www.thescotsmanhotel.com

SELF-CATERING

The Chester Residence £££ If you want five-star luxury without the hotel feel, these five apartments are the choice for you. Beautifully decorated with full attention to detail, you can cater for yourself but won't have to worry about clearing up as the apartments are

serviced daily. ⓐ 9 Chester Street ⓣ (0131) 226 2075
ⓦ www.chester-residence.com

Edinburgh Self-Catering ££–£££ This company provides
various apartments in the city centre, mostly in the Old Town.
ⓦ www.edinburgh-selfcatering.co.uk

YOUTH HOSTELS
There are two main youth hostels in Edinburgh. The Edinburgh
Eglinton is near Haymarket Station in the West End, while
Edinburgh Bruntsfield at Bruntsfield Crescent in the Bruntsfield
suburb is only a short bus ride from the city centre.
ⓦ www.syha.org.uk

CAMPING
Edinburgh Caravan Club Site To the north of the city on the Firth of
Forth, caravans and tents are both accepted in what is the most
convenient area for the city centre. ⓐ Marine Drive ⓣ (0131) 312 6874

Mortonhall Park This country estate has caravans to let and pitches
for tents, as well as communal bathing facilities, a laundry and a
games room. ⓐ 38 Mortonhall Gate, Frogston Road East
ⓣ (0131) 664 1533 ⓦ www.meadowhead.co.uk

Tantallon Caravan Park Outside the city at North Berwick is this
lovely park with sea views and a golf course. Both tent camping and
caravanning are available. ⓐ Dunbar Road, North Berwick
ⓣ (01620) 893 348 ⓦ www.meadowhead.co.uk

THE BEST OF EDINBURGH

If you only have a short time in Edinburgh, the best way to get a feel for the city is to take one of the many organised tours.

Auld Reekie Tours takes visitors through the city's haunted and underground history. ⓐ 45–47 Niddry Street ⓣ (0131) 557 4700 ⓦ www.auldreekietours.com

Edinburgh Tour Guides offers individual tours, either on foot or by car. ⓣ (0131) 443 0548 ⓦ www.edinburghtourguides.com

Lothian Buses organises hop-on hop-off bus tours of the city centre. ⓣ (0131) 220 0770 ⓦ www.lothianbuses.com/edinburghtours

TOP 10 ATTRACTIONS

- **Arthur's Seat**   Edinburgh was built on the site of an extinct volcano (see page 74).

- **Calton Hill**   This replica of the Greek Parthenon, high on a hill overlooking the New Town, confirmed Edinburgh's nickname 'Athens of the North' (see pages 86–7).

- **Edinburgh Castle**   Recently voted the most spectacular landmark in Britain, no visitor should miss the place where it all began (see pages 64–7).

- **Edinburgh International & Fringe Festival** The largest arts festival in the world takes over the city every August (see pages 14–15).

- **Edinburgh Military Tattoo** A spectacular performance by the Scottish regiments and international regimental guests in front of the castle every August (see page 10).

- **Museum of Scotland** Arguably the best museum in the country, it uncovers Scottish history from prehistoric times to the present day (see pages 76–7).

- **National Gallery of Scotland** A wonderful collection of fine art, both international and Scottish (see pages 91–2).

- **The Palace of Holyroodhouse** Still the official royal residence in Scotland, the highlight here is the apartments of Mary, Queen of Scots (see pages 70–1).

- **The Royal Mile** Leading from the castle to the palace, this cobbled street is the hub of the Old Town with innumerable sights along its route (see pages 71–3).

- **The Scott Monument & Princes Street** This bustling street offers the best view in the city (see pages 89).

Palace of Holyroodhouse

Your at-a-glance guide to seeing the best that Edinburgh has to offer, depending on how much time you have.

HALF DAY: EDINBURGH IN A HURRY

If you're pressed for time but want a little exploration, head straight for the Royal Mile, taking in the atmosphere of this medieval cobbled street, and walk up to the castle. Admire the views from the ramparts, marvel at its precarious clifftop position, then go inside to uncover the history of the Scottish monarchy and the city.

● *Views of the Forth from Arthur's Seat*

1 DAY: TIME TO SEE A LITTLE MORE

If you have more time, you can appreciate the two contrasting aspects of the city: the medieval and the Georgian. From the Royal Mile walk over North Bridge into Princes Street to admire the views and visit the National Gallery. Then walk around the streets behind it, such as George, Queen, Dublin and Dundas streets, to admire the Georgian architecture for which the city is so renowned.

2–3 DAYS: SHORT BREAK

Explore almost all aspects of this wonderful city. Enjoy a waterside drink in Leith and witness the successful regeneration of the once run-down docklands area. Take in the arty atmosphere of Stockbridge then stroll along the Water of Leith to Dean Village to visit the Dean Gallery and the wonderful work of the Scottish sculptor Eduardo Paolozzi. Weather permitting, walk up to the peak of Arthur's Seat to experience a taste of the wilderness right in the heart of the capital.

LONGER: ENJOYING EDINBURGH TO THE FULL

With added time you can either re-visit some of the areas to take in more sights, such as the National Portrait Gallery and the Botanic Gardens in the New Town or the Museum of Scotland and Royal Museum in the Old Town. Or take a journey out to the Borders and Firth of Forth region, enjoying the wildness of Gullane Beach or exploring the mysterious Rosslyn Chapel, 9 km (6 miles) south of the city.

Something for nothing

Edinburgh is not a particularly expensive city and entrance to all its museums is free, except for special exhibitions. However, there are plenty of other ways to take in the city without having to put your hand in your wallet.

The **National Library of Scotland** is the largest library in the country and is a fantastic collection of rare books, manuscripts, maps and other items relating to Scottish history and culture. Of

⬥ *Arthur's Seat*

particular interest is the collection of traditional Scottish music.
ⓐ George IV Bridge ☏ (0131) 226 4531 ⓦ www.nls.uk 🕐 10.00–17.00
Mon–Sat, 14.00–17.00 Sun; admission free

For those who like to walk, either through urban or natural
landscapes, few cities offer so many opportunities. Within the city
the Water of Leith (see page 90) is a lovely stroll along the riverbank
where various water birds can be spotted. The Royal Botanic
Gardens (see pages 89–90) are a draw for budding horticulturalists,
particularly in spring when the daffodils and many other plants
come into bloom. For those with a head for heights, climb to the top
of Calton Hill (see page 86) to see the Parthenon and the Nelson
Monument as well as great views of the New Town, or for a more
wild experience ascend Arthur's Seat (see page 73) and the Salisbury
Crags where, on a clear day, you'll have an enviable view across the
Forth to Fife.

Take advantage of Edinburgh's coastal location by either
exploring the urban style of The Shore in Leith or head out to
Portobello for a walk along the sandy beach, a favourite with the
city's dog owners.

THE EDINBURGH PASS

If you're only in the city for a short time and want to cram in
every sightseeing possibility it is worth buying the Edinburgh
Pass, available for one-, two- or three-day periods. Although it's
an initial cost, it does then gain you free bus travel and free
entrance into more than 25 attractions, including Our
Dynamic Earth (see page 70), themed tours and any special
exhibitions going on in the galleries or museums, as well as
discounts in many shops and restaurants.

When it rains

Sad to say, it's likely that most visitors will experience a spot of rain during a trip to Edinburgh, particularly in autumn and winter, but there are numerous attractions that are fascinating in their own right and that will protect you from outside downpours, aside from the various museums and galleries.

BRASS RUBBING CENTRE

Those with an artistic leaning can escape the weather by visiting the Trinity Apse on the Royal Mile and trying their hand at brass rubbing on the church's medieval brasses. Staff are in situ to show you what to do and if the bug bites, there are also kits on sale.
ⓐ Chalmers Close, High Street ① (0131) 556 4364 ⓒ 10.00–17.00 Mon–Sat Apr–Sept; noon–17.00 Sun Aug; admission free, but there is a charge to make a rubbing

CAMERA OBSCURA

The rooftop terrace may be outside, but inside the Camera Obscura are plenty of attractions displaying optical illusions and tricks, including holograms, 3-D images of Edinburgh, as well as the camera itself where you can 'spy' on the city in secret.
ⓐ Castlehill ① (0131) 226 3709 ⓒ 9.30–18.00 Apr–June & Sept–Oct; 9.30–19.30 July–Aug; 10.00–17.00 Nov–Mar; admission charge

THE REAL MARY KING'S CLOSE

Edinburgh's closes were high-rise tenement buildings with dire, cramped living conditions. For centuries the former homes lay hidden beneath the city but they have now been opened as a tourist attraction. Guides in costumes and character guide visitors through a series of dark, dusty chambers to reveal just how squalid life here could be, as well as narrating the story of some of the inhabitants.

ⓐ 2 Warriston's Close, High Street ⓣ (0870) 2430160
ⓦ www.realmarykingsclose.com ⓛ 10.00–21.00 Apr–Oct;
10.00–16.00 Nov–Mar; admission charge

SCOTCH WHISKY HERITAGE CENTRE

Very close to the Tartan Weaving Mill, the Scotch Whisky Heritage Centre uncovers the history of that other great Scottish tradition. There's a model distillery, a journey back in time via dioramas riding on a whisky 'barrel' on tracks, and an explanation of the different malt whiskies and where they are made. Perhaps most importantly there's a well-stocked shop where you can pick up a bottle or two to take home.

ⓐ 354 Castlehill ⓣ (0131) 220 0441 ⓦ www.whisky-heritage.co.uk
ⓛ 10.00–18.00; admission charge

TARTAN WEAVING MILL & EXHIBITION

As you'll see tartan adorning everything from teddy bears to slippers along the Royal Mile, step out of the rain and into the Tartan Weaving Mill to see how it's made. Watch the weavers at work at their power looms, learn about clan tartans and dress up in Highland costume, before deciding whether you want to buy some tartan to take home with you.

ⓐ 555 Castlehill ⓣ (0131) 226 1555 ⓛ 9.00–17.30 Mon–Sat, 10.00–17.30 Sun; admission free

On arrival

TIME DIFFERENCES

Edinburgh's clocks follow Greenwich Mean Time (GMT). During Daylight Saving Time (end Mar–end Oct) the clocks are put forward one hour. In the Scottish summer when it is 12 noon in Edinburgh, time elsewhere is as follows:

Australia Eastern Standard Time 21.00, Central Standard Time 20.30, Western Standard Time 19.00
New Zealand 23.00
South Africa noon
USA and Canada Newfoundland Time 08.30, Atlantic Canada Time 08.00, Eastern Time 07.00, Central Time 06.00, Mountain Time 05.00, Pacific Time 04.00, Alaska 03.00

ARRIVING

By air

Edinburgh International Airport is 12 km (8 miles) from the city centre and an efficient Air Link coach connects the two for the 20-minute journey. There are also plenty of taxis for a higher cost. There are flights between Edinburgh and London and many other British cities every day, as well as flights to many European cities. There is also a daily flight between Edinburgh and New York, but for more international flights Glasgow Airport, an hour away from Edinburgh, is a better option.

Many people are aware that air travel emits CO_2 which contributes to climate change. You may be interested in the possibility of lessening the environmental impact of your flight through the charity Climate Care, which offsets your

CO$_2$ by funding environmental projects around the world.
Visit www.climatecare.org

🔺 *One of the many statues adorning the castle esplanade*

By train

Train services into Edinburgh Waverley station are handled by the Great North Eastern Railway (GNER), Virgin and ScotRail. There are daily services between London and Edinburgh, making the four-hour journey, as well as direct links to York, Lancaster and Newcastle in England, and Aberdeen, Glasgow and Inverness in Scotland. To find

◐ *Waverley Station in the heart of the city*

out about timetables and fares contact National Rail Enquiries:
☎ (08457) 48 49 50 **ⓦ** www.nationalrail.co.uk

By coach

National Express coaches (**☎** (0870) 580 80 80
ⓦ www.nationalexpress.com) link Edinburgh with various UK and
Scottish cities and are a great budget option for getting to the city.

By car

Edinburgh is at the centre of a spider's web of motorways and
A roads, including the M1/A1 coastal route from London. Coming
from the west of England the M6/A74 is the best route to both
Edinburgh and Glasgow. The city is directly linked to Glasgow via
the M8. The journey time by road between London and Edinburgh
is about eight hours.

By sea

An overnight ferry (**ⓦ** www.superfast.com) operates between
Zeebrugge in Belgium and Rosyth, just north of the city centre with
a crossing time of 17 hours.

FINDING YOUR FEET

Edinburgh has recently been voted the safest city in Europe, so no
visitor should feel any sense of threat, although like everywhere, in
crowded tourist spots pickpockets may be in operation so keep an
eye on your belongings at all times. Traffic can be a problem in the
centre so use the pedestrian crossings, wait for the green man to
light up, and remember that traffic will be coming from the right
not the left. Policemen, taxi drivers and locals, who are invariably
friendly, will all help if you need to ask for directions.

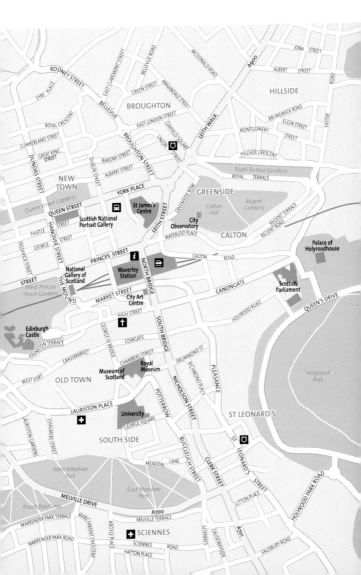

ORIENTATION

The majority of Edinburgh, bar Leith, is small enough to explore entirely on foot, although the bus service is excellent and taxis are plentiful. The city centre is divided between two areas, the Old Town and the New Town, separated by the North and Waverley railway bridges. The main thoroughfare of the Old Town is the Royal Mile (High Street), while New Town begins at the busy Princes Street. The 'villages' of Dean Village, Stockbridge and Inverleith are easily reached by bus from the New Town. The easiest way to reach Leith is to take a bus or taxi along the long stretch known as Leith Walk. It's almost impossible to get lost around the tourist areas of the city but good landmarks to head for, should you become separated from friends or family, are the Scott Monument on Princes Street and the Tron church on the Royal Mile.

GETTING AROUND

As previously mentioned, walking is one of the best ways to see Edinburgh, to take in the many views and soak up the atmosphere of this buzzing city. But for saving on shoe leather or for those with mobility issues, there are many other ways to get around.

Buses

There is no subway system in Edinburgh so the bus network is crucial to the city's infrastructure and runs a comprehensive and reliable service. Glass-sheltered bus stops are in abundance, and will have a plan of the route each numbered bus will take. Selected stops on the route are also written on the front of the bus. Single-day bus passes are available or you can pay for single fares but you must have the exact change. A standard single fare in the city is currently 80 pence. The main bus station in Edinburgh is on St Andrew Square in the

New Town, from where you can take buses to the Borders, around the city, and to many other places around Scotland.

For more information on routes and other details contact **Lothian Buses** ☎ (0131) 555 6363 🌐 www.lothianbuses.co.uk

Taxis

Black cabs are in plentiful supply on Edinburgh's streets and can be hailed from the pavement if their yellow For Hire light is on. Most taxi drivers are friendly and helpful and love to talk about their city with tourists. Fares are metered and the cost is shown on a light above the driver's windscreen. At the end of your journey pay the driver through the glass cavity between the driver's and passenger's compartment. It's customary to offer a small tip, particularly if the cabbie has been particularly friendly and skilled at avoiding main road traffic. The limit of passengers per taxi is five people.

There are also various companies that you can telephone to order a taxi from your location:
Central Taxis ☎ (0131) 229 2468
ComCab ☎ (0131) 272 8000
City Cabs ☎ (0131) 228 1211

Driving

Traffic can be heavy in Edinburgh and parking restrictions are rife so driving is not the most sensible option. If you do want to drive, however, make sure you understand the parking regulations, use pay and display ticket machines and never park on double yellow lines or red routes. Traffic wardens abound and are very keen on writing tickets.

If you're just coming into Edinburgh for the day, en route to other destinations, Lothian Buses (🌐 www.lothianbuses.com) operate a

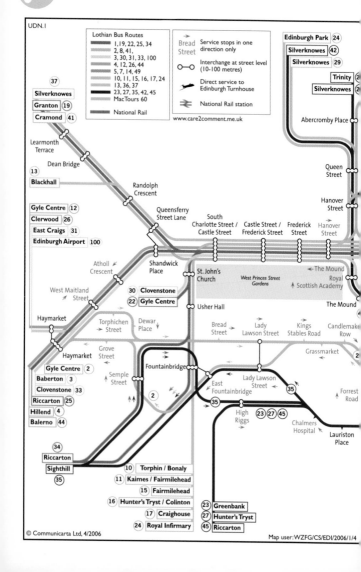

UDN.1

Lothian Bus Routes
- 1, 19, 22, 25, 34
- 2, 8, 41,
- 3, 30, 31, 33, 100
- 4, 12, 26, 44
- 5, 7, 14, 49
- 10, 11, 15, 16, 17, 24
- 13, 36, 37
- 23, 27, 35, 42, 45
- MacTours 60

National Rail

Bread Street → Service stops in one direction only

O—O Interchange at street level (10-100 metres)

✈ Direct service to Edinburgh Turnhouse

⇌ National Rail station

www.care2comment.me.uk

Edinburgh Park 24
Silverknowes 42
Silverknowes 29
Trinity 2
Silverknowes 2

37
Silverknowes
Granton 19
Cramond 41

Abercromby Place

Learmonth Terrace

Dean Bridge
13
Blackhall

Randolph Crescent

Queen Street

Queensferry Street Lane

Hanover Street

Gyle Centre 12
Clerwood 26
East Craigs 31
Edinburgh Airport 100

South Charlotte Street / Castle Street

Castle Street / Frederick Street

Frederick Street

Hanover Street

Shandwick Place

Atholl ✈ Crescent

St. John's Church

West Princes Street Gardens

← The Mound

Royal Scottish Academy

West Maitland Street ✈

30 Clovenstone
22 Gyle Centre

Usher Hall

The Mound

Haymarket

Torphichen → Street

Dewar ↓ Place

Bread Street →

Lady Lawson Street

Kings Stables Road

Candlemaker Row

Grove Street

Grassmarket

Haymarket

Gyle Centre 2
Baberton 3
Clovenstone 33
Riccarton 25
Hillend 4
Balerno 44

Semple Street

Fountainbridge

East Fountainbridge

Lady Lawson Street ←

35

Forrest Road ↑

2

35

High Riggs

23 27 45

Chalmers Hospital ✈

Lauriston Place

34
Riccarton
Sighthill
35

10 Torphin / Bonaly
11 Kaimes / Fairmilehead
15 Fairmilehead
16 Hunter's Tryst / Colinton
17 Craighouse
24 Royal Infirmary

23 Greenbank
27 Hunter's Tryst
45 Riccarton

© Communicarta Ltd, 4/2006

Map user: WZFG/CS/EDI/2006/1/4

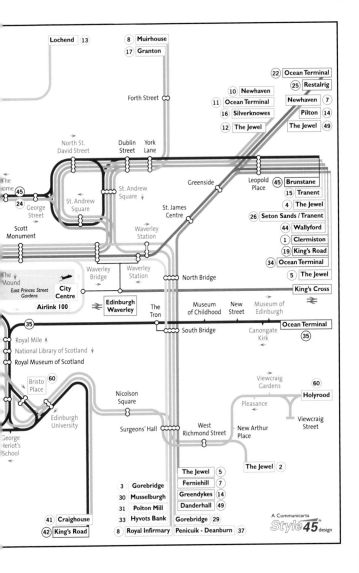

useful Park and Ride scheme, where you can park your car at two places outside the centre – Ingliston and Hermiston – then take a bus into the heart of the city.

CAR HIRE

Hiring a car certainly isn't necessary if you are only going to explore the city, but to reach the outlying areas, this can be a convenient way to get around. As well as multinational chains such as Avis and Hertz there are several Edinburgh-based car hire options. Costs obviously vary between companies, but the average cost for an economy size car is £30 for a day and £150 for a week's hire.

Avis

Wide range of cars, including people carriers and one-way rentals are possible, dropping the car off at another Avis office. ⓐ 5 West Park Place (off Dalry Road), Haymarket ⓣ (0131) 337 6363 ⓦ www.avis.co.uk

Condor Self Drive

Edinburgh's top car and van hire centre. Special weekend rates available and a free pick-up service. ⓐ 45 Lochrin Place, Tollcross ⓣ (0131) 229 6333 ⓦ www.condorselfdrive.co.uk

Edinburgh Self Drive

Special weekend rates and 24-hour roadside assistance are part of their deals. ⓐ 45 Lochrin Place ⓣ (0131) 229 8686 ⓦ www.edinburghselfdrive.co.uk

Thrifty Car Rental – Edinburgh

Another multinational chain known for its good value. Drivers must be between 23 and 70 years of age. ⓐ 42 Haymarket Terrace ⓣ (0131) 337 1319 ⓦ www.thrifty.co.uk

▶ *The Dean Gallery is home to the work of Eduardo Paolozzi*

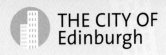

Old Town

Edinburgh has innumerable 'neighbourhoods' that can often change name from street to street, but its most clear divisions are between the Old Town and the New Town. It is the Old Town to which most tourists are drawn, for its medieval heritage, cobbled streets, haunted histories and the spectacular castle, all of which have earned it a World Heritage Site status. The Royal Mile acts as a logical spine to the area, linking the castle with the wilderness that is Arthur's Seat and sprouting numerous interesting branches east and west of this renowned thoroughfare. The whole area is easily explored on foot, although the cobbles are unforgiving to high heels or unsturdy shoes.

SIGHTS & ATTRACTIONS

Cowgate

The area below the Royal Mile, known as Cowgate, is the Old Town's primary nightlife area with an array of clubs and bars and, at weekends in particular, rowdy drunken partygoers. It's also the location for cheap hostel accommodation, so most of the revellers don't have far to stagger at the end of the evening. The famous Edinburgh fire of 2002 began in this area and destroyed the much-loved Gilded Ballroom Comedy Club. Rebuilding work can still be seen, but the fire was fortunately put out before the blaze spread to the rest of the Old Town.

Edinburgh Castle

Perched high on a volcanic crag above the city, Edinburgh's castle is the capital's most famous and important sight. Home to the

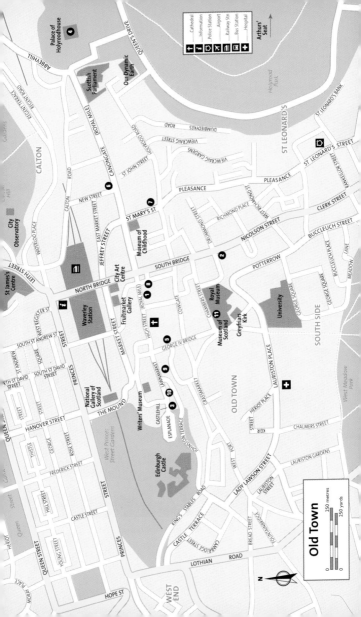

Scottish monarchy until the 17th century when James VI became James I of England, the castle has a long history of conflict between the English and the Scots. The oldest surviving part of the castle (and Edinburgh) today is St Margaret's Chapel, dating from the 12th century. Also on the site is the Scottish National War Memorial, erected to remember all the Scots who gave their lives in World War I, and subsequent conflicts. A tour of the interior of the castle gives a detailed view of the history of the Scottish monarchy, including the troubled journey of the Honours of the Kingdom

⬥ *The Palace of Holyroodhouse remains an official royal residence*

(the Scottish Crown Jewels) culminating with a chance to look at this spectacular regalia behind heavily secured glass. Also in the castle is the Stone of Destiny (also known as the Stone of Scone). This square-shaped stone on which Scottish kings were traditionally crowned was stolen by King Edward I of England in 1296 and housed in Westminster Abbey, but was finally returned to Scotland, with much ceremony, in 1996. The Great Hall is also impressive for its vaulted ceiling and displays of historic weaponry and armour.

On the ramparts two cannons are popular attractions. The 15th-century Mons Meg is a siege gun presented to James II by the Duke of Burgundy, and the One O'Clock Gun is still fired every Monday to Saturday as a time signal. From here there are wonderful views across to the New Town, along Princes Street and up to Calton Hill.

Also on the castle grounds is the National War Museum of Scotland, where centuries of Scottish military activities are explored and illustrated with documents, uniforms and many other items. The castle is still a working military base, home to the Royal Scots Regiment, the Royal Scots Dragoon Guards and Royal Military Police.
ⓐ Castle Hill ⓣ (0131) 225 9846 ⓦ www.historic-scotland.gov.uk
ⓛ 9.30–18.00 Apr–Oct; 9.30–17.00 Nov–Mar; admission charge

Greyfriars Kirk

This Old Town church is of great historical significance in Scotland as it was the first city church to be built after the Reformation and, more importantly, it was here that the National Covenant of 1638 was signed, marking the beginnings of the Presbyterian faith. Some 40 years later, in 1679, more than 1,000 Covenanters were imprisoned in the graveyard for three months, during which time many of them died from hunger. The area is now a museum and the Martyrs Monument commemorates those that perished. Many well-known names have their burial place here, including the architects John Adam and James Craig, and the poet Allan Ramsay. Many graves also still bear metal protective measures against the bodysnatching trend of the 19th century, in particular Burke and

GREYFRIARS BOBBY

In 1858 an Edinburgh policeman by the name of John Gray passed away and was buried in Greyfriars Kirk. He left behind a devoted Skye terrier called Bobby, who pined for his master so much that he kept a vigil at his graveside for 14 years until he himself died at the age of 16. After unsuccessful attempts to remove the dog, the keeper of the churchyard gave him shelter and, in time, the sight of Bobby on his master's grave became the stuff of local legend. People would come specifically to see the dog, particularly at the time of the One O'Clock Gun when he would go to the same coffee house he had frequented with Gray and be given his midday meal. By 1867, when a law was passed requiring all dogs to be licensed, Bobby had become so famous that the Lord Provost of Edinburgh paid for his licence himself and the collar indicating this is now in the Museum of Edinburgh (see page 72). In 1873, a year after Bobby died, a granite statue in his memory and in recognition of his devotion was erected opposite the churchyard, and can still be seen today, at the end of Chambers Street, in front of a pub also named in his honour. The story of Bobby has touched the heart of many over the years, and has been turned into a feature film numerous times.

▶ *A statue commemorates the most loyal dog in the world*

Hare. The churchyard is best known, however, as the resting place of John Gray, master of Greyfriars Bobby.

Our Dynamic Earth

One of Edinburgh's most unique attractions, and perennially popular with children, is the large exhibition centre at the base of the Royal Mile, dedicated to exploring and understanding the planet Earth. From prehistoric landscapes to images of the Earth's core, the exhibits also cover diverse climatic zones from tropical rainforest to Antarctic icebergs and volcanic regions. Various special exhibitions are held throughout the year, focussing on topics such as Scottish geology.

ⓐ Holyrood Road ⓣ (0131) 550 7800 ⓦ www.dynamicearth.co.uk
ⓛ 10.00–17.00 Wed–Sun Nov–Feb; 10.00–17.00 Apr–Oct (until 18.00 July–Aug); admission charge

The Palace of Holyroodhouse

Still the official royal residence in Scotland and a setting for state occasions, the Palace of Holyroodhouse was established as a monastery in 1128. After Edinburgh was declared the capital of Scotland in 1460 the abbey was converted into a palace by King James IV, moving the monarchy to this more attractive parkland and away from the castle. It is best known as the home of Mary, Queen of Scots (see page 120), who lived in the palace between 1561–7, and was also the setting for the famous and mysterious murder of her private secretary David Rizzio by her husband Lord Darnley. Her private apartments have been preserved as they were in her day. The palace fell into decline during Cromwell's reign, but Charles II, who held his coronation here, oversaw many renovations including creating the Chapel Royal, and much of the Baroque detail dates from this time. In the 19th century further renovations were made when Queen Victoria returned to the tradition of using the palace as a royal residence when in Scotland. Ceremonial activities are largely carried out in the Great Gallery, lined with 89 portraits of Scottish kings by the artist Jacob de Wet, while each June and July the Queen holds a Holyrood Garden Party here.

ⓐ Canongate, Royal Mile ❶ (0131) 556 5100 ❷ 9.30–18.00 Apr–Oct; 9.30–4.30 Nov–Mar; admission charge ❶ May be closed during official occasions, so phone ahead for details

The Royal Mile

Officially called High Street, Lawnmarket, Canongate and Castlehill, the Royal Mile is thus nicknamed because of the route it takes between the castle and the Palace of Holyroodhouse. One of the most famous streets in Britain, its cobbled length throngs with tourists year round, soaking up the atmosphere of tartan shops, the occasional bagpiping busker and a string of largely unimpressive cafés and restaurants. Starting from the castle end the Tartan Weaving Mill and the Scotch Whisky Heritage Centre are well placed to trap tourists into buying two of the country's most enduring symbols (see page 51). Nearby is Tollbooth Kirk, also known as The Hub because it's where tickets for the Edinburgh Festival are now sold, boasting the tallest spire in the city. Further down are Parliament Square and the High Kirk of St Giles. On the pavement in front of Parliament Square is a heart-shaped stone known as the Heart of Midlothian, on the site of the former Tollbooth. Spitting on the stone is supposed to bring good luck and a promised return to the city, even if the superstition is a little uncouth. The High Kirk of St Giles was instrumental in the establishment of the Presbyterian Church of Scotland, but today is notable for its stained-glass windows and an ornate chapel added to

⬤ *The new Scottish Parliament building*

the church in 1911. Almost opposite the church, beneath the City Chambers, is The Real Mary King's Close (see pages 50–51). Further down, still on the same side of the road as St Giles, is the Tron Kirk, dating from 1637, and now home to a tourist information centre. Inside there are also views of excavations of the cellars that began in the 1970s and offer a fascinating insight into underground Edinburgh centuries ago. The church gets its name from the Tron, a public weighing machine for merchants, which was once sited here. Almost opposite the Museum of Childhood (see page 76) is John Knox House, a quirky 15th-century building that is now a museum dedicated to the life and work of Knox, the Calvinist leader and a great inspiration in the forming of the National Covenant and the Presbyterian Church. Two museums dedicated to local city life sit opposite each other on the area of the Mile known as Canongate. The Museum of Edinburgh has various displays recounting the history of the city, including Greyfriars Bobby's dog collar and the National Covenant of 1638, while The People's Story is a more evocative exhibition detailing the squalid and impoverished conditions endured by citizens in the 18th and 19th centuries. Rooms such as a prison cell, a wash house and a pub are recreated with historical detail while tales are told through oral observations from characters such as a fishwife, a servant and a merchant.

John Knox House ❷ 43–45 High Street ❶ (0131) 556 9579
🕐 10.00–16.00 Mon–Sat, noon–17.00 Sun; admission charge

Museum of Edinburgh ❸ 142 Canongate ❶ (0131) 529 4143
🕐 10.00–17.00 Mon–Sat, noon–17.00 Sun; admission free

The People's Story ❷ 163 Canongate ❶ (0131) 529 4057
🕐 10.00–17.00 Mon–Sat, noon–17.00 Sun; admission free

ARTHUR'S SEAT

One of the most unique aspects of the city of Edinburgh is that it is sited on the landscape of extinct volcanoes, the most notable of these being the area known as Arthur's Seat, the looming mass that can be seen from many vantage points in the city. It's a popular spot for hikers, especially in summer, when views of Edinburgh, Fife and even the Highlands reward those who manage to reach the 250-m (822-ft) peak. It is also a chance to sample a piece of real Scottish wilderness without even having to leave the capital. Surrounding the peak is Holyrood Park, another popular day out for nature lovers in the heart of the city. The source of the name is unclear, but it is thought to relate to King Arthur, who was renowned as a legendary warrior among military outposts that were once located here. On the other side of the peak is Duddingston Village, an attractive enclave of Edinburgh boasting the country's oldest pub (see page 82) and a pretty bird-filled loch.

The Scottish Parliament Building

One of the most controversial buildings in modern Edinburgh history is the Scottish Parliament, designed by the Spanish architect Enric Miralles. There are many reasons for the debate: the choice of a foreign architect was unpopular; the cost of the building escalated far beyond the proposed budget, which many Edinburghers felt should have been spent elsewhere; and the futuristic design, including a roof that is supposed to reflect up-turned fishing boats, was not felt to be in keeping with the rest of the Old Town landscape. It has, however, won many architectural awards after it opened in 2004, including the Stirling Prize in 2005. Although Scotland was governed by the Parliament in London for almost 300 years, there was a long push for devolution, and the Scottish Parliament was finally established in 1998. While matters of national importance are still governed by Westminster, the Scottish Parliament has a limited amount of power over domestic issues such as agriculture, health and some tax issues, such as council tax. It also oversees the Scottish Executive, the Scottish branch of the civil service.

ⓐ Canongate ⓣ (0131) 348 5200 ⓦ www.scottish.parliament.uk
Visitor Centre: ⓛ 9.00–19.00 Tues & Thur, 10.00–18.00 Mon & Fri (until 16.00 Nov–Mar), 10.00–16.00 Sat & Sun; admission free

CULTURE

City Art Centre

The City Art Centre is best known for its regularly changing temporary exhibitions that have covered themes as diverse as

---

❶ *Spires like these are typical of the Royal Mile*

Egyptology and *Star Trek*. Within its permanent collection are some of the city's finest Scottish works, including the Scottish colourists, sculpture and photography.

a 2 Market Street **t** (0131) 529 7902 **c** 10.00–17.00 Mon–Sat, noon–17.00 Sun; admission free

Fruitmarket Gallery

If conceptual art is your thing, including art installations, large-scale sculpture, videos and all manner of the weird and the wonderful, then you're likely to enjoy whatever current exhibit is on at the Fruitmarket Gallery. There's also an excellent art bookshop here, and a lovely café.

a 45 Market Street **t** (0131) 225 2383 **w** www.fruitmarket.co.uk
c 11.00–18.00 Mon–Sat, 11.00–17.00 Sun; admission free

Museum of Childhood

As much a nostalgic treat for adults as it is a fascinating step back in time for children, different areas of this eclectic museum gather together toys from days gone by, including a doll gallery, train sets, board games and penny arcades. There's also a set of historic dioramas, including a pre-war schoolroom and a Victorian parlour, as well as many interactive opportunities on each level, such as a puppet show and a dressing-up box.

a 42 High Street **t** (0131) 529 4142 **c** 10.00–17.00 Mon–Sat, noon–17.00 Sun; admission free

Museum of Scotland

Without doubt the best museum in the country, the Museum of Scotland traces the full history of the country from prehistoric times to the present day. Of particular interest are the areas exploring

Gaelic Scotland, the Jacobite uprising led by Bonnie Prince Charlie, exploration into the production of tartan and paisley cloth, and the effects of the Industrial Revolution, including original steam engines and a whisky distillery.

ⓐ Chambers Street ☏ (0131) 247 4422 ⓦ www.nms.ac.uk
🕒 10.00–17.00 Mon–Sat, noon–17.00 Sun; admission free

Royal Museum

Set within a spectacular galleried Victorian building, the focus of the Royal Museum is on science and discovery, as well as decorative arts. The Natural World area examines wildlife and geology, with a special emphasis on Britain, while the cultural areas illustrate influences from around the world, including a highly informative gallery devoted to ancient Egypt. The most popular part of the museum, however, is that devoted to science and industry, with many interactive exhibits, a history of the many Scottish innovators such as Alexander Graham Bell, and a fascinating collection of objects from 1850 to the present day illustrating the advances in art and design. The building is linked to the Museum of Scotland by a covered walkway.

ⓐ Chambers Street ☏ (0131) 247 4422 ⓦ www.nms.ac.uk
🕒 10.00–17.00 Mon–Sat, noon–17.00 Sun; admission free

The Writers' Museum

Scotland has produced many well-known writers, but three stand out as world-class literary figures: Robert Burns, Sir Walter Scott and Robert Louis Stevenson. This museum, set in a lovely turreted 17th-century house, focuses on their three individual careers and includes many of their personal items including Burns' writing desk and Stevenson's riding boots. Regular temporary exhibitions also pay homage to other Scottish writers of note. Outside the museum is a courtyard bearing quotations by a variety of Scottish authors.

ⓐ Lady Stair's Close ☎ (0131) 529 4901 🕐 10.00–17.00 Mon–Sat, noon–17.00 Sun; admission free

RETAIL THERAPY

The Royal Mile is the place to head for if you're after touristy souvenirs, including everything in tartan, from umbrellas to dressed up teddy bears. Royal Mile Whiskies is an emporia of more than 1,000 malt whiskies, which make welcome gifts for friends back home partial to a tipple. For smokers, The Cigar Box is a treasure trove of Cuban cigars, Zippo lighters and other smoking paraphernalia. For good quality Scottish jewellery, particularly Celtic designs, head further down the road to The Tappit Hen. Nearby is Geoffrey Kiltmakers where you can get your own kilt made up in your choice of tartan, as well as find numerous accessories associated with Highland dress. Just off the Royal Mile, Cockburn Street is the heart of hippiedom in Edinburgh, with tattoo parlours, and second-hand clothes and record stores. In the Grassmarket area is one of Edinburgh's most unusual shops, Mr Wood's Fossils, specialising in fossils and minerals from around the world.

Royal Mile Whiskies ⓐ 379–381 High Street ☎ (0131) 225 2283
The Cigar Box ⓐ 361 High Street ☎ (0131) 225 3534
The Tappit Hen ⓐ 89 High Street ☎ (0131) 557 1852
Geoffrey Kiltmakers ⓐ 57–59 High Street ☎ (0131) 557 0256
Mr Wood's Fossils ⓐ 5 Cowgatehead, Grassmarket
☎ (0131) 220 1344

Scottish Power Edinburgh Farmers' Market
Every Saturday, in the shadow of the castle, farm producers from
all over Scotland gather to sell their home-reared specialities,
such as venison, wild boar, fish and seafood, as well as speciality
Scottish cheeses, chutneys and oatcakes.
ⓐ Castle Terrace ⓛ 9.00–14.00 Sat

TAKING A BREAK

Always Sunday £ ❶ A popular café right on the Royal Mile,
serving breakfasts, cakes, lunchtime snacks, fruit smoothies and
Fair Trade coffee. ⓐ 170 High Street ⓣ (0131) 622 0667
ⓦ www.alwayssunday.co.uk ⓛ 8.00–18.00 Mon–Fri, 9.00–18.00
Sat & Sun

Black Medicine Coffee Company £ ❷ An Italian coffee shop
serving delicious cakes and panini sandwiches as well as, of course,
top quality Italian espressos and cappuccinos. ⓐ 2 Nicolson Street
ⓣ (0131) 622 7003 ⓛ 8.00–20.00 Mon–Sat, 9.00–20.00 Sun

Cafe Hub £ ❸ Evocatively set within a renovated part of the
Tolbooth Kirk, this is an ideal brunch setting near the castle.
ⓐ Castlehill ⓣ (0131) 473 2067 ⓦ www.thehub-edinburgh.com
ⓛ 10.00–23.00

Café At The Palace £ ❹ Conveniently located for a visit to
the Palace of Holyroodhouse, this lovely café serves hot and
cold drinks and light snacks during the opening hours of the
palace (see pages 70–71). ⓐ Palace of Holyroodhouse, Canongate
ⓣ (0131) 556 5100

● *Whisky is Scotland's national drink*

Elephant House £ ❺ A perennially popular snack stop, serving a variety of coffees and snacks such as bagels and sandwiches. More than 600 miniature elephants decorate the crowded location.
ⓐ 21 George IV Bridge ❶ (0131) 220 5355 ❷ 9.00–18.00

Plaisir du Chocolat £ ❻ This elegant Parisian-style tea salon makes a great refreshment stop for warming coffee and hot chocolate on cold days or iced tea on warmer days. Snacks and French classics such as *croque monsieur* and *moules marinières* are also served.
ⓐ 251–253 Canongate ❶ (0131) 556 9524
ⓦ www.plaisirduchocolat.com ❸ 9.00–18.00

AFTER DARK

Restaurants
David Bann Restaurant £ ❼ A top choice for vegetarians in the city, this restaurant takes the hippie stigma out of vegan and vegetarian food with dishes such as walnut, hazelnut and mushroom haggis. ⓐ 56–58 St Mary's Street ❶ (0131) 556 5888
ⓦ www.davidbann.com ❸ 11.00–01.00

Creelers ££ ❽ One of the finest seafood restaurants in the city, just by the Tron Kirk. Owners Tim and Fran James import fish and seafood directly from their own smokehouse on Arran and serve it all with simplicity and a great deal of bonhomie.
ⓐ 3 Hunter Square (just off High Street) ❶ (0131) 220 4447
❸ noon–14.00 Mon–Sun, 17.30–22.30 Sun–Thur, 17.30–23.00 Fri & Sat
❶ Closed Tues & Wed lunch Nov–May

Howies ££ ❾ There are four Howies restaurants in Edinburgh and this site in the historic heart of the Old Town is located very close to the Royal Mile. Dishes include such warming options as venison casserole with root vegetables. ⓐ 10–14 Victoria Street
❶ (0131) 225 1721 ⓦ www.howies.uk.com ❸ noon–14.30, 18.00–22.30

The Witchery by the Castle ££ ⑩ Considered by many to be the best restaurant in Scotland, this dark, atmospheric place at the foot of the castle offers such Scottish specialities as wild salmon, fillet of beef and oysters all served with style and imagination. A favourite celebrity hang-out for both local and visiting luminaries. ⓐ Castlehill ⓣ (0131) 225 5613 ⓦ www.thewitchery.com ⓛ noon–16.00, 17.30–23.30

The Tower £££ ⑪ Beautifully decorated in a contemporary yet cosy style with great views of the castle and the city, the menu here concentrates on seasonal Scottish produce, including oysters, game and fish. As it's part of the Museum of Scotland, it's not a place for a late night dinner, but a wonderful end to a day of sightseeing in the Old Town. ⓐ Museum of Scotland, Chambers Street ⓣ (0131) 225 3003 ⓦ www.tower-restaurant.com ⓛ noon–19.00

Pubs & Bars

The Royal Oak A little more touristy than Sandy Bell's, The Royal Oak is nevertheless an Edinburgh stalwart, also known for its folk music that is a little more rowdy and participatory than Bell's. ⓐ Infirmary Street (off South Bridge) ⓣ (0131) 557 2976

Sandy Bell's This tiny, rather drab bar has earned itself an international reputation for its nightly live folk music, largely provided by students under the helm of friendly fiddler Freddie. ⓐ Forrest Road (off Lauriston Place) ⓣ (0131) 225 2571

The Sheep Heid Inn Claiming to be the oldest pub in Scotland, with past clientele allegedly being Mary, Queen of Scots and Bonnie Prince Charlie, it may well be true. Located in the pretty 'village' of Duddingston (at the rear of Arthurs' Seat), it still draws regulars from the city centre, who come for its good food, eclectic décor and famous skittle alley. ⓐ 43–45 Causeway, Duddingston ① (0131) 656 6951

The Waverley A small, highly traditional Edinburgh pub with an arty, intellectual atmosphere. A great place to come for a quiet drink away from the nearby tourist traps on the Royal Mile. Traditional ales, more than 70 malt whiskies and a friendly if laconic barman. ⓐ St Mary's Street ① (0131) 556 8855

Live Music & Clubs

The Bongo Club A café and dance studio by day, the Bongo Club comes alive at night with a mixture of live music and DJs, varying between punk, hip hop, reggae and other beats. ⓐ 37 Holyrood Road ① (0131) 558 7604 ⓦ www.thebongoclub.co.uk

The Honeycomb Set in an atmospheric vaulted underground area, the Honeycomb is an Edinburgh clubbing institution that has been going strong for over 20 years. DJs blend with multimedia and sound and light displays. ⓐ 15–17 Niddry Street (off South Bridge) ① (0131) 556 2442 ⓦ www.the-honeycomb.com

The Liquid Room One of the Old Town's best live music venues, recent artists performing here have included KT Tunstall and the Kaiser Chiefs. For clubbers there's also weekly indie nights and monthly house music nights. ⓐ 9c Victoria Street (near Castlehill) ① (0131) 225 2564 ⓦ www.liquidroom.com

New Town

Edinburgh's Old Town may be the main tourist draw for its historic sights, but it is the New Town that gives the city its much deserved reputation for elegance. The word 'New' is a bit of a misnomer these days, as the area dates from the 18th century, but compared to the medieval alleys and lanes up by the castle, these wide avenues and curving circuses must have seemed very new indeed. Much of the New Town owes its Georgian splendour to the architect James

⬧ *View of the castle from Princes Street Gardens*

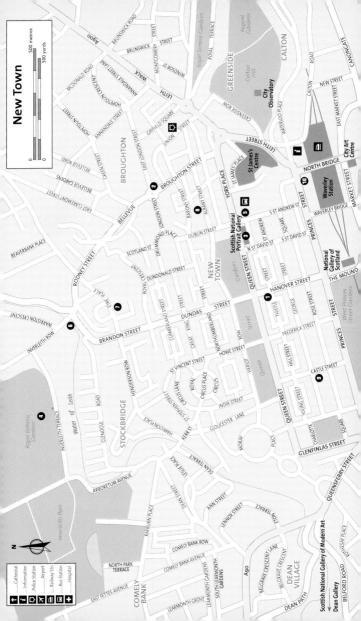

Craig, who was commissioned to create homes for the city's wealthy. Although very few of these are private houses today, instead converted into flats or offices, their external gracefulness has still been preserved. Another architect, Robert Adam, also made an impression on this part of the city with the design of areas such as Charlotte Square. Today the New Town is considered the hub of Edinburgh, where most of the fashionable bars and restaurants are located, as well as designer shops, and there's a palpable sense of money in the air.

SIGHTS & ATTRACTIONS

Broughton Street

This is purportedly the heart of Edinburgh's gay community, although there's little sign of it as you stroll this short, steep street. Rather it's a lovely collection of quirky boutiques, one-off cafés and old-fashioned pubs such as The Barony (see page 98). On the north corner is the enormous neo-Norman Mansfield Place Church, inside which are beautiful murals by the Arts and Crafts artist Phoebe Traquair. After years of neglect and damage from seeping water, the murals are currently undergoing an extensive restoration programme.

Calton Hill

Edinburgh is often described as the 'Athens of the North', a term enhanced by its replica Parthenon, looming down over the city from its position on Calton Hill. The folly is officially known as the National Monument, and was constructed by the architect Charles Cockerell, a great Greek Revivalist, in 1824 as a commemoration of soldiers killed during the Napoleonic Wars. Also on the hill are Nelson's Monument, honouring the great admiral in the shape of a telescope, and an observatory. Great views of the city can be had from the hilltop, but for even further reaching views across to Fife, climb the telescope to take in the panorama.

Charlotte Square

This square is considered by many to be the *pièce de résistance* of the architect Robert Adam, who designed the square in the late 18th century. Today it suffers somewhat from being a heavy traffic artery, but the quality of the architecture can still be seen. West Register House was originally a church, influenced by St Paul's Cathedral, and the headquarters for the National Trust for Scotland at No 28 has had its façade lovingly restored to its original 18th-century appearance. At No 7 is the Georgian House, built in 1796, and now preserved as a living example of the elegance of that age. Run by the National Trust for Scotland, various elements, such as paintings, furniture and silverware are on display, giving a great insight into the lives of Edinburgh's aristocracy in Georgian times.

Georgian House ☎ (0131) 226 3318 🕐 10.00–17.00 Apr–Oct; 10.00–15.00 Nov–Mar; admission charge

Dean Village

To the west of the New Town is the charming and peaceful area known as Dean Village. Once a milling area that was separated from the city centre, it now makes for a pleasant stroll, particularly along the Water of Leith. Old mills and warehouses can still be seen, some of which have been turned into much sought after flats, and in all the atmosphere is quite at odds with the bustling capital just a few minutes away. Dean Village is also a must for art-lovers, as it's the location for the Scottish National Gallery of Modern Art (see page 92) and the Dean Gallery (see page 91).

Princes Street

When most people think of Edinburgh, the image that immediately comes to mind is bustling Princes Street and its spectacular view up to the castle and the Old Town, earning the capital the title 'City of Spires'. The street marks the division between the Old Town and the New Town, separated by bridges and the railway track that runs into Waverley Station. Although the street is an extremely popular shopping street, the outlets here are standard to most British high streets and lack the exclusivity of areas such as George Street (see page 93). The main draw here, apart from the view, are the Princes Street Gardens. Formerly a city lake, the Nor' Loch, it was filled in during the 18th century when it had become overrun with sewage, and replaced by gardens, which are particularly attractive in winter when a Christmas market and funfair take place here. Near the station end of the street is the impressive **Scott Monument**, dedicated to the revered Scottish writer Sir Walter Scott. Designed in 1844 by George Kemp, a statue of Scott is framed by a number of characters from his novels, beneath a 60-m (197-ft) high Gothic arch. In the Princes Street Gardens West, don't miss the Floral Clock, the oldest of its kind in the world, replanted every year.

Royal Botanic Gardens

Begun in the 17th century, these 30 hectares (74 acres) of land in the area of Inverleith are a stunning oasis of green in the city, particularly on a sunny spring day when the new flowers are coming into bloom. Although its main role is as a scientific research centre, it is nevertheless one of the city's major visitor attractions,

◐ *The tropical Glasshouse in the Royal Botanic Gardens*

with a rock garden, a Chinese garden, a tropical Glasshouse, an orchid house, an aquatic house with rainforest specimens, and many other divided areas. The Terrace Café is a great place for an outdoor lunch or drink in summer, and the views of the city from the gardens' hilltops are some of the best in Edinburgh.

ⓐ 20A Inverleith Row ☏ (0131) 552 7171 ⓦ www.rbge.org.uk
🕐 10.00–19.00 Apr–Sept; 10.00–18.00 Oct & Mar; 10.00–16.00 Nov–Feb; admission free, although there is a charge to enter the Glasshouses

Stockbridge

A few minutes' walk from central New Town and you enter a whole new atmosphere in the village-like area of Stockbridge. Long known as the arty, bohemian side of the city, its main charm lies in its small art galleries, antiques shops, specialist food shops and smart wine bars and coffee shops. Slightly further along is Comely Bank, the setting for that great novel of Edinburgh snobbery *The Prime of Miss Jean Brodie*, while the fantastical building of Fettes College, which counts Tony Blair among its alumni, could well have been the inspiration for Harry Potter's Hogwarts school, with its baronial turrets and eerie style.

Water of Leith

The Water of Leith flows for 35 km (22 miles) from the Pentland Hills, outside the city, to the Leith waterfront, meandering through the west of the city on its path. The most attractive part of the waterside is the path around Dean Village and Stockbridge, which is popular with cyclists, dog walkers and people just out for a stroll. The river was a vital source of industry in times gone by when it helped drive waterwheels for the paper, flour and wool mills along its route, but this also meant that it was heavily polluted. Today, however, much wildlife including trout and minnows flourishes here.

CULTURE

Dean Gallery

While the Old Town is the part of the city to head for to discover excellent museums, the New Town is the home of Edinburgh's great art collections. One of the newest galleries is the Dean Gallery in Dean Village, opened in 1999 in a former hospital building specifically to house the work of the great Scottish sculptor Eduardo Paolozzi, including the huge robotic figure, but is also home to an impressive Surrealist collection, including works by Salvador Dalí and Pablo Picasso. One of the most popular areas of the gallery is the re-created artist's studio of Paolozzi, filled with models, books and all manner of inspirational objects. The gallery also holds regular temporary exhibitions featuring specific artists or artistic schools, such as the Scottish colourists. There's also an excellent and very popular café within the building.

ⓐ 73 Belford Road ⓣ (0131) 624 6200 ⓒ 10.00–17.00 Fri–Wed, 10.00–19.00 Thur; admission free

National Gallery of Scotland

For those with a more classic taste in art, this gallery, just off Princes Street, is the one to head for. Unlike many of its equivalents in other cities, it is of a very manageable size so you shouldn't experience art fatigue. The oldest gallery in Edinburgh, dating from 1859, it's home to a fine collection of Renaissance and Impressionist works, including masters such as Gauguin, Tiepolo, El Greco and Botticelli. Furthermore, the gallery shouldn't be missed by anyone with a keen

interest in Scottish art. Among its most famous paintings is the *Reverend Robert Walker Skating on Duddingston Loch* (1795) by Sir Henry Raeburn, which has become something of a symbol of the city. Various temporary exhibitions are also staged throughout the year, including a display of Turner watercolours every January.
ⓐ The Mound ☎ (0131) 624 6200 🕙 10.00–17.00 Fri–Wed, 10.00–19.00 Thur; admission free

Scottish National Gallery of Modern Art

Across the road from the Dean Gallery, with gardens decorated by sculptures by such luminaries as Henry Moore and Barbara Hepworth, the Scottish National Gallery of Modern Art focuses on art from the late 19th century onward. Among the works are those by René Matisse, Francis Bacon, Andy Warhol and Lucien Freud, but the most famed collection is that of the Scottish colourists such as Sir William Gillies and Joan Eardley.
ⓐ 75 Belford Road ☎ (0131) 624 6200 🕙 10.00–17.00 Fri–Wed, 10.00–19.00 Thur; admission free

Scottish National Portrait Gallery

Unsurprisingly all the portraits in the Scottish National Portrait Gallery's permanent exhibition are of eminent Scots, although visiting temporary exhibitions carry a broader theme. Among those immortalised on canvas are Mary, Queen of Scots, Robert Burns and Sir Walter Scott and, more recently, Sean Connery and the football manager Sir Alex Ferguson. There are also sculptures here, a photography collection and a numismatic collection of coins. The gallery's building is a star in its own right – an impressive 19th-century neo-Gothic sandstone edifice on the outside, and decorated with beautiful murals depicting the history of Scotland on the inside.

ⓐ 1 Queen Street ❶ (0131) 624 6200 ❷ 10.00–17.00 Fri–Wed,
10.00–19.00 Thur; admission free

RETAIL THERAPY

George Street

While Princes Street may be the most famous shopping street in
Edinburgh, George Street, running parallel behind it, is certainly the
most elegant. Not so much designer names but high-end fashion
chains such as LK Bennett, Coast, Hobbs and Karen Millen are to be

⬤ *Sculpture in the gardens of the Scottish National Gallery of Modern Art*

found here. There are also two large book chains here, Ottakar's and Waterstone's, and the street is lined with classy bars and coffee shops for when you're in need of refreshment.

Harvey Nichols

London's most exclusive department store opened its Edinburgh branch to much ceremony in 2002, and it is now the landmark of Multrees Walk, a pedestrianised walkway lined with designer names such as Louis Vuitton and Armani. Come here for a sense of luxury in toiletries, clothing and a superb foodmarket, as well as an overpriced but panoramic restaurant on the fourth floor. ⓐ 30–34 St Andrew Square ⓣ (0131) 524 8388 ⓦ www.harveynichols.com

Jenners

The *grande dame* of Edinburgh's department stores, Jenners is traditional in style, service and products, but popular nonetheless. It has occupied its prime Princes Street site since 1838, but was recently taken over by the House of Fraser group, losing its once independent status. All the usual department store goods can be found here, but it's particularly strong on Scottish-produced items. ⓐ 48 Princes Street ⓣ (0131) 225 2442 ⓦ www.jenners.com

Princes Street

Come here for the bustle and the views rather than the quality of the shopping, which is primarily made up of downmarket chains selling fashion, electrical goods and other paraphernalia that can be found on any high street in the country. At the western end, however, is House of Fraser, one of the city's other main department stores.

▶ *The Water of Leith is at its best in Stockbridge and Dean Village*

St James's Centre

The eyesore that is the St James's Centre, which ruins the rest of this area's style, may soon be removed as it was sold to a developer in 2005. For the time being, however, it's a convenient stop for everyday items and cheap fashion, and it also benefits from a branch of John Lewis. ⓐ Princes Street ⓣ (0131) 557 0050 ⓛ 9.00–18.00 Mon–Sat, 11.00–17.00 Sun

TAKING A BREAK

Henderson's Salad Table £ ❶ A self-service vegetarian restaurant with a deli and takeaway facilities too. A great lunch choice, even if you're a committed carnivore. ⓐ 94 Hanover Street ⓣ (0131) 225 2131

The Lost Sock Diner £ ❷ The food's nothing special here – the usual diner-style burgers and sandwiches – but come for the novelty of a café/diner attached to a working launderette. ⓐ 11 East London Street ⓣ (0131) 557 6097

Queen Street Café £ ❸ If you're in need of afternoon refreshment, you can do no better than the cakes and scones at the Scottish National Portrait Gallery's café. ⓐ 1 Queen Street ⓣ (0131) 557 2844

Terrace Café £ ❹ If you're visiting the Royal Botanic Gardens and it's a sunny day, don't miss the opportunity to soak up the warmth and the views from the lovely Terrace Café. Seating inside and out. ⓐ Inverleith Row ⓣ (0131) 552 0616

Vin Caffè £–££ ❺ A recent addition to Valvona & Crolla's flagship store on Leith Walk (see pages 102–103), the Vin Caffè does sell a small selection of the famous Italian produce, but it is mainly a café and restaurant. Downstairs are more informal sandwiches and snacks sold from a glass-fronted counter, while upstairs is a smart but reasonably priced restaurant serving excellent Italian cuisine. A great lunch spot if you're taking in a bit of the retail opportunities of George Street and St Andrew Square. ③ Multrees Walk ① (0131) 557 0088

AFTER DARK

Restaurants
Loon Fung £–££ ❻ Considered by many to be the best Chinese restaurant in the city, this stalwart specialises in dim sum and a range of other Cantonese dishes that aren't regularly seen on most Chinese menus. ③ 2 Warriston Place ① (0131) 556 1781

Duck's at Le Marché Noir ££ ❼ Scallops, Aberdeen Angus beef and sea bass risotto are just some of the delicious offerings at this established Edinburgh restaurant. ③ 14 Eyre Place ① (0131) 558 1608 ⓦ www.ducks.co.uk

Haldanes ££ ❽ Scottish cuisine is the order of the day at this well-known Edinburgh eatery. ③ 39a Albany Street ① (0131) 556 8407

Oloroso ££ ❾ One of the city's finest restaurants and a celebrity favourite, with a stylish dining room combining classic white tablecloth elegance with a modern feel. The roof terrace has great views of the castle, even more atmospheric when floodlit at night. The à la carte menu changes daily and there's also a grill menu. ③ 33 Castle Street ① (0131) 226 7614 ⓦ www.oloroso.co.uk

Number One £££ ❿   This Michelin-starred restaurant within The Balmoral hotel (see page 40) is renowned for its superb cuisine using the best of Scottish produce. Try the hare and rabbit terrine, or the roasted guinea fowl with braised cabbage. ⓐ 1 Princes Street ❶ (0131) 557 6727

Pubs and bars

The Barony Like the Café Royal, the Barony is known for its Victorian tiles and authentic atmosphere. It does get crowded, but for good reason, and there's a mixed crowd. Live music on Sundays. ⓐ 81–85 Broughton Street ❶ (0131) 557 0546

Café Royal Possibly the best-known pub in Edinburgh, with a quietly sedate air about it (apart from Friday nights when it fills up with after-work drinkers). Both the bar and the adjoining restaurant are renowned for their oysters, while the Victorian tiling and long wooden bar add to the ambience. ⓐ 17a West Register Street (off Princes St) ❶ (0131) 556 4121

Clark's Bar The place to come if you're into real ale – there are five of them here, as well as a large selection of malt whiskies. Very popular among its locals and a very traditional Scottish feel. ⓐ 142 Dundas Street ❶ (0131) 556 1067

Hector's A stylish wine bar in the Stockbridge area, generally appealing to the younger end of the drinking market, but that's not to say it's rowdy. A refined, arty kind of atmosphere – an ideal place to read the Sunday papers over a glass of wine. ⓐ 47–49 Deanhaugh Street (near Raeburn Place) ❶ (0131) 343 1735

The Oxford They rarely come more traditional than this. Made famous by Ian Rankin's Rebus crime novels, as this was the watering hole of choice for the fictional inspector, expect sparse décor, a collection of old cronies drinking and chatting at the tiny bar and creaky chairs in a small upstairs back room. But then that's what gives it its appeal. ⓐ 8 Young Street ⓣ (0131) 539 7119

LIVE MUSIC & CLUBS

Ego One of the most popular clubs in the New Town, with different themed nights including Disco Inferno, Wiggle (gay night) and the very popular Vegas. ⓐ Picardy Place (top end of Leith Walk) ⓣ (0131) 478 7434

The Jam House Jools Holland's live music venue opened in 2005 and has proved a great hit. There's music every night, from mellow jazz and blues before 10pm to more lively music into the early hours. Food is also served. Over 21s only, and no trainers allowed. ⓐ 5 Queen Street ⓣ (0131) 226 4380 ⓦ www.thejamhouse.com

The Living Room A restaurant, bar and live music (blues and jazz) venue in the heart of the New Town. The food is simple but nicely presented. ⓐ 113–115 George Street ⓣ (0870) 4422 718 ⓦ www.thelivingroom.co.uk

The Venue A long-standing Edinburgh club, with the most popular gay night, Joy, in the city. Well-known guest DJs also play here frequently as do smaller-scale pop bands. ⓐ 17–21 Calton Road ⓣ (0131) 557 3073

Leith & the waterfront

For many years Leith was the blot on Edinburgh's landscape – a run-down, working-class neighbourhood of abandoned docks that saw itself as apart from the rest of the city. Indeed, even today, Leithers are very proud of their individualism from the rest of the Edinburghers. In the 1980s, however, a regeneration programme was set in place and parts of Leith have since become some of the most fashionable parts of the city, particularly along The Shore area, where designer hotels and great pubs and restaurants line the waterfront. Do be careful in side streets after dark, however – it's not all rejuvenated just yet. It's easy to forget, when you're engrossed in the sights of the city centre, that Edinburgh is a coastal town, and further along are the lovely seaside 'villages' of Portobello and Musselburgh to the east and Newhaven to the west, which make ideal locations for a Sunday walk if the sun has happened to come out.

SIGHTS & ATTRACTIONS

Commercial Quay

This former dock has now been converted into an atmospheric street complete with pond and fountain and lined with canopied restaurants. The entrance to the quay is marked by a sculpture of a fish and a boat to recall the city's fishing heritage. Also here is the Scottish Executive building, home to the country's civil service. At weekends there is a covered market here selling antiques, second-hand clothes, books and more.

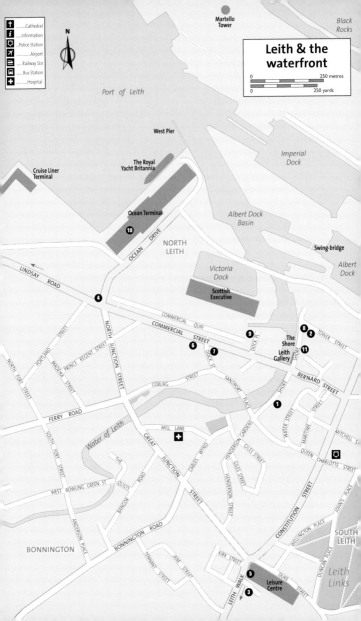

Leith & the waterfront

Cathedral
Information
Police Station
Airport
Railway Stn
Bus Station
Hospital

N

0   250 metres
0   250 yards

Black Rocks

Martello Tower

Port of Leith

Imperial Dock

West Pier

The Royal Yacht Britannia

Cruise Liner Terminal

Ocean Terminal

10

Albert Dock Basin

Swing-bridge

Albert Dock

OCEAN DRIVE

NORTH LEITH

LINDSAY ROAD

4

Victoria Dock

Scottish Executive

COMMERCIAL QUAY

COMMERCIAL STREET

9

DOCK PLACE

The Shore

Leith Gallery

8 **2**

TOWER STREET

11

6

7

DOCK ST

SANDPORT PLACE

COBURG STREET

BERNARD STREET

SHORE

WATER STREET

1

MARITIME STREET

MITCHELL ST

NORTH JUNCTION STREET

PORTLAND STREET

PRINCE REGENT STREET

MADEIRA STREET

NORTH FORT STREET

FERRY ROAD

Water of Leith

MILL LANE

✚

HENDERSON GARDENS

GILES STREET

GILES STREET

HENDERSON STREET

QUEEN CHARLOTTE STREET

JOHN'S PLACE

SOUTH FORT STREET

THE SHORE

QUILTS

BANGOR ROAD

CABLES WYND

GREAT JUNCTION STREET

CONSTITUTION STREET

WELLINGTON PLACE

DUNCAN PLACE

SOUTH LEITH

WEST BOWLING GREEN ST

ANDERSON PLACE

BONNINGTON

BONNINGTON ROAD

TENNANT STREET

JANE STREET

KIRK STREET

LEITH WALK

5

3

Leisure Centre

DUKE STREET

Leith Links

Leith Links

Although St Andrews often claims to be the birthplace of golf, it was at Leith Links, now a public park, that the game was first recorded in the 15th century, and by the 18th century it was home to a five-hole course. The official rules of golf, which are still followed today, were settled here in 1744 by the Honourable Company of Edinburgh Golfers during the first ever golfing competition.

Leith Walk

This long thoroughfare of bustling shops, pubs and Indian fast-food restaurants links the city centre with Leith, ending at what is known as the Foot o' the Walk. There's not much by way of attractions here,

○ *A mural in Leith depicts the working class roots of the area*

but it's interesting to take in the change of atmosphere between the top of the walk (where there's a statue of Sherlock Holmes to commemorate Arthur Conan Doyle's birthplace at Picardy Place) and the foot, to see the clear distinction between Leith and the rest of the city.

Musselburgh

Just 9 km (6 miles) to the east of Edinburgh, Musselburgh is a lovely fishing village that lays claim to being Scotland's oldest town. This may well be, as it was founded by the Romans in AD 80. Today it is best known for sports such as the Musselburgh Race Course (see page 36), as well as an excellent golf course which took over from Leith Links in the 19th century when larger courses were needed.

Newhaven

To the west of Leith is the small area known as Newhaven, which for centuries was an important naval and fishing base. A heritage museum in the area tells the history of these two aspects, set within the former fish market building. Old photographs, documents and fishermen's and fishwives' costumes are among the exhibits. On a clear day there are also lovely views of Fife from here.

Newhaven Heritage Museum @ Pier Place ☎ (0131) 551 4165 ⏰ noon–16.45; admission free

Portobello

Eight kilometres (5 miles) east of the city, Portobello is a slightly run down seaside 'village' that was extremely popular with Edinburgh aristocracy in the 18th and 19th centuries. In summer it's usually crowded with families and dog walkers and makes a nice escape from the centre, with amusement arcades, ice cream vendors and

mini fair rides. The area was once famous for its potteries industry, which was closed in 1929, although the kilns can still be seen. The historic Portobello Baths were built in 1901 and once were filled with sea water, although today chlorinated fresh water is used. Many original features of the building can still be seen.

The Royal Yacht *Britannia*

From 1953 to 1997 The Royal Yacht *Britannia* served the Royal Family on numerous trips and cruises around the world and is now permanently moored at Ocean Terminal. Apart from the restaurants and bars of the area, it's the main tourist draw for Leith and has done much to bolster the area's reputation. Inside, visitors can see the royal cabin-apartments, which are surprising in their homely feel, filled with personal memorabilia and family mementoes, and the great contrast of the grandeur of the state dining room. The yacht was also used for various royal honeymoons, including that of the Prince and Princess of Wales who sailed around the Mediterranean for their trip. There's also plenty of information about the lives of the crew and their many duties, from the trivial to the arduous, and tours of the mess, the sick bay, the engine room and the bridge.

ⓐ Ocean Terminal ⓣ (0131) 555 5566

ⓦ www.royalyachtbritannia.co.uk ⓛ 9.30–16.30 Apr–Oct; 10.00–15.30 Nov–Mar; admission charge

The Shore

The main focus of Leith's regeneration, The Shore is today a quaint area of restaurants, arty shops, luxury apartment blocks, and

◐ *The Royal Yacht* Britannia *is a major boon to the area*

quirky sculpture that gives a nod to Edinburgh's seafaring past. It's particularly attractive on a sunny day when the many bars and cafés lay out pavement tables and you can enjoy a drink on the waterfront. Historically this port area saw the export of coal and salt, while Baltic pine was imported here from Europe. Whaling was also handled from here from the 17th century. The Signal Tower was used to guide ships into the port through a system of flags.

CULTURE

Leith Gallery

This award-winning gallery is one of the best places in the city to see Scottish contemporary art, both established and up and coming.

TRAINSPOTTING

One of Scotland's most renowned modern-day writers is Irvine Welsh, who made his debut with the novel *Trainspotting* in 1993. Set largely in Leith in the 1980s, prior to its regeneration, it tells the tales of a group of heroin addicts in one of the worst drug enclaves in Britain. The stream-of-consciousness style, combined with the heavy use of Scots dialect, made for difficult reading for mainstream audiences, but the characters of Begbie, Sick Boy, Renton and others soon captured the public's imagination and it was nominated for the Man Booker Prize. The book was then translated into a play, and from that came a highly successful film, which made stars out of Scottish-born actors Ewan McGregor and Robert Carlyle. Many locations that feature in the film, such as the Central Bar (see p110) can still be visited. Tours of the area related to the book and the film can also be booked. ☎ (0131) 554 3568

It stages a regularly changing programme of temporary exhibitions on all themes, including sculpture, ceramics and jewellery.

ⓐ 65 The Shore ☎ (0131) 553 5355 🕒 11.00–17.00 Mon–Fri, 11.00–16.00 Sat; admission free

RETAIL THERAPY

Diana Forrester

An ideal place for gifts, particularly bath time goodies and other luxury items for the home. ⓐ 54 Constitution Street ☎ (0131) 554 4651 ⓦ www.dianaforrester.co.uk

Flux

Specialising in Scottish crafts but with plenty of other gift items too, including nicely designed cards, many of which are handmade.

ⓐ 55 Bernard Street ☎ (0131) 554 4075

Ocean Terminal

The smartest shopping mall in the city is also one of Leith's biggest draws. Designed by Sir Terence Conran, more than 75 outlets, including Debenhams, Earth Squared for home interiors, Waterstone's and French Connection make their home here. There's also a 12-screen cinema and elegant restaurants, including Conran's own Zinc (see page 110). ⓐ Ocean Drive ☎ (0131) 555 8888

Relish

A wonderful delicatessen not far from The Shore, with food and wine from all over the world and a superb collection of cheeses. There's also a small café at the front of the shop selling coffee and snacks. ⓐ 6 Commercial Street ☎ (0131) 476 1920

Valvona & Crolla

First opened in 1934, this Italian deli has become an Edinburgh institution. Absolutely everything you could wish for in the way of Italian cuisine, from hams and salamis, cheeses, superb olive oil, breads and wines can be found here. There's also an on-site café-bar, so you can sample the produce while you shop. ⓐ 19 Elm Row, Leith Walk ⓣ (0131) 556 6066

TAKING A BREAK

Café Truva £ ❶ Turkish mezes, cakes, coffee and apple tea are all available from this specialist café. ⓐ 77 The Shore ⓣ (0131) 554 5502

Malmaison £ ❷ Whether you're after a light lunch or just a drink, the bar of this well-known hotel (see page 39) makes for an elegant refreshment stop. ⓐ 1 Tower Place ⓣ (0131) 468 5000

Valvona & Crolla £ ❸ For a mouth-watering bowl of spaghetti or a freshly baked pizza you can't go wrong with the Caffè Bar inside this famous deli's premises (see above).

AFTER DARK

Restaurants

Britannia Spice £ ❹ One of the best Asian restaurants in the city, with speciality dishes from India, Thailand, Nepal and Sri Lanka, all served with elegant finesse. ⓐ 150 Commercial Street ⓣ (0131) 555 2255 ⓛ noon–14.00 & 17.00–23.45 Mon–Sat, 7.00–23.45 Sun

---

⊙ *One of the smart contemporary restaurants in Ocean Terminal*

Central Bar £ ❺ Architecturally one of the most attractive pubs in Edinburgh, with Victorian tiling and stained-glass windows.
ⓐ 7 Leith Walk ❶ (0131) 467 3925

Daniel's Bistro £ ❻ A friendly relaxed atmosphere and both French and Scottish cuisine make this a popular Leith hang-out.
ⓐ 88 Commercial Street ❶ (0131) 553 5933 ❷ noon–22.00

International Starters £ ❼ A novel idea, serving a menu consisting entirely of starters, following cuisine from different parts of the world. The American menu includes fried chicken wings and Mexican tacos, while the Asian menu includes chicken satay and bhajis. ⓐ 82 Commercial Quay ❶ (0131) 555 2546 ❷ 17.00–22.00 Mon–Fri, noon–15.00, 17.00–22.00 Sat, 12.30–20.00 Sun

The Shore ££ ❽ The restaurant here specialises in local seafood in an elegant wood-panelled dining room. Next door is the pub, which is always crowded and often features live jazz. ⓐ 3 The Shore ❶ (0131) 553 5080 ⓦ www.theshore.biz ❷ noon–14.30, 18.30–22.00

Skippers ££ ❾ Right next door to The Waterfront, this is the best seafood restaurant in Leith, the menu changing daily according to the catch. ⓐ 1a Dock Place ❶ (0131) 554 1018 ⓦ www.skippers.co.uk ❷ 12.30–14.00, 19.00–22.00 Mon–Sat, closed for lunch Sun

Zinc Bar and Grill ££ ❿ Set within the Ocean Terminal shopping centre (see page 107), Terence Conran's restaurant serves fresh local food from an open-plan kitchen and has the added benefit of views over the water to Fife. ⓐ Ocean Terminal, Ocean Drive ❶ (0131) 553 8070 ❷ noon–22.00 Sun–Thur, noon–23.00 Fri & Sat

Restaurant Martin Wishart £££ ⑪ Leith's only Michelin-starred restaurant serves a wonderful French-inspired menu of seafood, game and Scottish beef. Book well in advance. ⓐ 54 The Shore ① (0131) 553 3557 ⓦ www.martin-wishart.co.uk ⓛ noon–14.00 Tues–Fri, 18.45–21.30 Tues–Sat

⬥ *Restaurants line the attractive Shore in Leith*

Pubs & bars

The Lighthouse The preserve of the young, this is the trendiest bar in Leith. It won Scotland's Style Bar of the Year award in 2004. ⓐ 32–34 The Shore ⓣ (0131) 554 9465

Old Chain Pier A Newhaven favourite, this pub is built on an old sea wall and has spectacular views to Fife. The food offers standard pub fare such as steak and kidney pie and fish and chips, as well as local seafood, depending on the catch. ⓐ 32 Trinity Crescent ⓣ (0131) 553 1233 ⓘ Food served noon–21.00 Mon–Sat, 12.30–20.00 Sun

Port 'O Leith One of Leith's best-known pubs, once a favourite with sailors and dockers and still decorated with seafaring memorabilia including flags and figureheads. ⓐ 58 Constitution Street ⓣ (0131) 554 3568

The Ship Another former dockers' pub, the rejuvenation of the area now makes this a pleasant place for a drink. ⓐ 24 The Shore ⓣ (0131) 555 0409

The Waterfront Combining a cosy bar with wooden booths and an excellent wine list with a fine waterside bistro set in a conservatory, this is one of Leith's tucked away jewels. Particularly strong on fish dishes. ⓐ 1c Dock Place ⓣ (0131) 554 7427 ⓦ www.waterfrontwinebar.co.uk ⓛ noon–23.00

◗ *Gateway to Hopetoun House*

The Firth of Forth

Temptingly close to the centre of Edinburgh, the 60-km (40-mile) coastline of the Firth of Forth and East Lothian beckons visitors with a range of purpose-made attractions, activities, historic sights and coastal landscapes. Portobello and Musselburgh are Edinburgh's own seaside suburbs (see page 103), while the coast grows increasingly wild and windswept as you head east towards the North Sea. Long beaches and stretches of sand dunes and the gannet-haunted Bass Rock and other islands of the Forth estuary are on the horizon. This stretch of coastline has been the scene of many battles, from Roman times through to Cromwell's defeat of Montrose's Royalists at Dunbar to the last Jacobite victory at Prestonpans in 1745, and is studded with romantic ruins. Regional buses from Edinburgh's St Andrew's Square bus station (see page 58) take around 40 minutes to get to Gullane. Frequent trains (at least one every hour) connect Edinburgh Waverley with Musselburgh, Prestonpans and North Berwick (a journey time of around 30 minutes), and Dunbar (around 45 minutes). If you're driving, the main A1 is the fast track to Haddington and Dunbar, while the A198 meanders along the coast through Prestonpans, Gullane and Dirleton to North Berwick.

SIGHTS & ATTRACTIONS

Anstruther

This pretty fishing village is mostly popular in summer when tourists come for the lovely beaches and the golfing. Another attraction is the Scottish Fisheries Museum in which the history of the area's fishing industry is uncovered via photographs, model boats and fishing gear.

Scottish Fisheries Museum ⓐ Harbourhead ⓣ (01333) 310 628
ⓦ www.scotfishmuseum.org ⓛ 10.00–17.30 Mon–Sat, 11.00–17.00
Sun, Apr–Sept; 10.00–16.30 Mon–Sat, noon–16.30 Sun, Oct–Mar;
admission charge

Dunbar

Built of red sandstone that glows warmly when the sun shines,
Dunbar was once a thriving North Sea port defended by a
medieval castle. The castle is now a ruin, and the picturesque
harbour is now home to more yachts and cruisers than fishing
vessels, but Dunbar is still an attractive little town and a pleasant
place to stop on a tour of the Lothian coast or the Borders, with
some good hotels, restaurants and pubs. Just north of town, the
sands and crags of Belhaven Bay and the Tyne estuary form part of
the John Muir Country Park, named after the Dunbar-born
conservationist who founded one of the world's first national parks,
Yosemite, after emigrating in the 19th century to California. You can
visit his birthplace, on the High Street, and find out more about
Dunbar's illustrious past at the neighbouring **Dunbar Museum**.

Dunbar's famous Belhaven Brewery can sadly no longer claim to
be Scotland's oldest independent brewhouse following its takeover
in 2005 by Greene King, but it still makes a fine pint and tours offer
a rare chance to visit a working brewery – and taste its products.
Dunbar Tourist Information Centre ⓐ 143A High Street ⓣ (01368)
863 353 ⓦ www.dunbar.org.uk
Belhaven Brewery ⓐ Dunbar ⓣ (01368) 869 200
ⓦ www.belhaven.co.uk ⓛ Tours Mon–Fri, book in advance;
admission charge

ⓞ *The Forth Bridge connecting Edinburgh with Fife*

Dunbar Museum ⓐ Town House, High Street, Dunbar ⓣ (01620) 828 203 ⓦ www.eastlothian.gov.uk/museums ⓛ 10.00–17.00 Mon–Sat, 13.00–17.00 Sun; admission free

John Muir's Birthplace ⓐ 126 High Street ⓣ (01368) 865 899 ⓦ www.jmbt.org.uk ⓛ 10.00–17.00 Mon–Sat, 13.00–17.00 Sun; admission free

Forth Bridges

Probably the most spectacular two bridges in Britain, the Forth Rail Bridge and the Forth Road Bridge straddle the watery expanse at parallel positions to each other. Prior to the rail bridge opening in 1890 a regular ferry plied the Forth between the Lothians and Fife, but the bridge considerably opened up the rest of Scotland to the rest of Britain. Fifty-seven men were killed during the construction of the cantilever crossing. Today it is Scotland's largest listed building. With the advent of heavier road traffic, it then became clear in the 20th century that another bridge for cars was needed, and the Forth Road Bridge was opened in 1964, at the time the longest suspension bridge in Europe. It remains a toll bridge on the northbound route, still trying to recoup its more than £19 million construction costs.

Gullane

With its wild sweep of sandy beach and huge views out to sea, the stretch of coast between Yellowcraig and Gullane is the most breathtaking section of the Firth's south shore and the perfect place for a windy walk to sweep away the cobwebs of a night on Edinburgh's tiles.

Gullane's sandy dunes make superb golf courses, and nearby Muirfield is renowned as one of Scotland's finest – despite the resolutely archaic, men-only rules of its governing body, the Honourable Company of Edinburgh Golfers.

Gullane Golf Club ❶ (01620) 842 255 ❼ www.golfeastlothian.co.uk; admission charge

Muirfield Golf Course, Gullane: ❶ (01620) 842 123 ❼ www.golfeastlothian.co.uk

Haddington

This pretty county town on the banks of the River Tyne has a wealth of postcard-pretty 17th- and 18th-century houses, churches and small local shops and pubs. Nearby are a range of historic attractions, including Lennoxlove House, home of the Duke of Hamilton, and Traprain Law, a 221-m (725-ft) extinct volcano and a superb natural fortress which is the site of one of the oldest Bronze Age strongholds in Europe, with panoramic views of the surrounding countryside.

Much more modern is the Museum of Flight, at a former RAF airfield about 6km (4 miles) from Haddington. This annex of the National Museum of Scotland boasts Britain's best collection of outstanding military and civil aircraft, including one of the last of the UK's supersonic Concorde airliners.

Museum of Flight ❷ East Fortune Airfield ❶ (01620) 880 308 ❼ www.nms.ac.uk ❹ 10.00–17.00 Apr–Oct; 11.00–16.00 Sat & Sun Nov–Mar; admission charge

Linlithgow

The picturesque town of Linlithgow is best known for its palace, the birthplace of both James V and Mary, Queen of Scots, set on its own loch and in extensive parkland. Now partly a ruin, the great hall and chapel are still impressive. Also in Linlithgow is the 17th-century

stately home known as the House of the Binns, once home to the Dalyells family. The house is filled with antiques and portraits, and is well worth a visit for anyone interested in the history of architecture.

MARY, QUEEN OF SCOTS

Born in 1542, Mary became Queen of Scots when she was just six days old and she was a pawn in English and Scottish politics for the rest of her life. The Scots initially betrothed her to Henry VIII's son Edward in an attempt to unite the two countries. However, after Catholic objections and to Henry's rage, they then changed their mind in favour of France, sending her to the French royal court as the future wife of the Dauphin Francis at the age of six. She and the Dauphin became King and Queen of France in 1558 but when the king died two years later, Mary returned to Scotland as monarch. It was her second marriage, however, to her cousin Lord Darnley that set the stage for her last tragic years. An unpopular and irascible man, Darnley murdered Mary's private secretary David Riccio in 1566 at the Palace of Holyroodhouse; when he was murdered a year later many people questioned whether Mary, or her third husband the Earl of Bothwell, were responsible. By this time her Protestant subjects had grown tired of their Catholic queen and she was imprisoned at Lochleven Castle, abdicating the throne in favour of her young son James. In the hope that Elizabeth I would be an ally, she fled to London where she was incarcerated for 19 years and finally executed in 1587 to put paid to the constant threat of Catholic ambitions. James VI of Scotland then became James I of England on the death of Elizabeth I.

Linlithgow Palace ☎ (01506) 842 896 🕒 09.30–18.00 Apr–Sept; 09.30–16.00 Mon–Sat, 14.30–16.30 Sun Oct–Mar; admission charge
House of the Binns: ☎ 01506 834 255 🕒 14.00–17.00 Sat–Thur June–Sept; admission charge

North Berwick

North Berwick is a pretty town with a sweep of sandy beach that – before the advent of cheap package holidays to the Mediterranean – made it one of Scotland's premier seaside resorts. It's still a very

🔺 *Gullane beach*

attractive place for a day out. With several good hotels, restaurants and guest houses, North Berwick is also a good base for an overnight stay while exploring East Lothian. Just outside North Berwick, Dirleton Castle is the cute ruin of a miniature stronghold

⬥ *Dirleton Castle*

set in traditional formal gardens and surrounded by what is claimed to be the world's longest herbaceous border – at least, according to the *Guinness World Records*. A grimmer and more formidable-looking castle lies 5 km (3 miles) east of North Berwick, on a vertigo-inducing clifftop site at Tantallon. A stronghold of the Douglases – one of the great dynasties of medieval Scotland – Tantallon defied many sieges until the advent of artillery, and the era of peace with England, made it redundant, and it's now one of the region's most spectacular and evocative ruins.

In summer, North Berwick is the base for boat trips to the Bass Rock, a windswept, craggy islet about 1 km (^{1}/2 mile) offshore, that guards the mouth of the Firth of Forth. Until the 18th century, this was an island fortress, defended by ramparts and batteries of cannon, and was also used as a prison for opponents of the Crown – Scotland's equivalent of Alcatraz. Today, its fortifications demolished long ago, the 108 m (350 ft) crag is deserted except for huge flocks of nesting gannets, guillemots, puffins, razorbills, fulmars and kittiwakes. Those too timid to enjoy the boat trip can watch the birds live on the cameras of North Berwick's newest attraction, the Scottish Seabird Centre, which show views of the Rock's seabird colonies and seal breeding sites.

North Berwick Tourist Information Centre ❷ 1 Quality St
❶ (01620) 892 197 ⓦ www.north-berwick.co.uk
Dirleton Castle ❷ 5 km (3 miles) west of North Berwick on A198
❶ (01620) 850 330 ❸ 09.30–16.30; admission charge
Scottish Seabird Centre ❷ The Harbour, North Berwick ❶ (01620) 890 202 ⓦ www.seabird.org ❸ 10.00–18.00 Apr–Oct; 10.00–16.00 Mon–Fri, 10.00–17.30 Sat & Sun, Nov–Mar; admission charge
Tantallon Castle ❷ 4 km (2.5 miles) east of North Berwick on A198
❶ (01620) 892 727 ❸ 09.30–16.30 Sat–Wed; admission charge

Prestonpans

Just outside Musselburgh (see page 103), Prestonpans was the scene of Bonnie Prince Charlie's first (and only) victory over King George's redcoats in 1745, and later became a centre of the mining industry. A kilometre south of Musselburgh is the site of the Battle of Pinkie. This famous defeat for the Scots in 1547 caused the death of King James V and the ascent to the throne of his young daughter, the ill-fated Mary, Queen of Scots, although today there is little left to see. More interesting, and redolent of the region's more recent history, is Prestongrange Museum, dedicated to the coal-mining industry that prospered in East Lothian from the 18th century until the 1980s. Highlights include a Cornish beam engine – one of the earliest steam engines – and the Power House, a museum and gallery with a calendar of temporary exhibitions.

Old Craighall Tourist Information Centre (off A1): ❶ (0131) 653 6172 Ⓦ www.eastlothianattractions.co.uk

Prestongrange Museum ❷ Morrison's Haven, Prestonpans ❶ (0131) 653 2904 ❹ 11.00–16.00 Apr–Oct

ACTIVITIES

Golf

The Forth coast claims to be the birthplace of golf (although that claim is disputed both by St Andrews, across the Firth on the Fife shore, and Leyden in the Netherlands). There are 19 top-quality courses around the East Lothian region – some of them legendary around the world – and many are open to visiting golfers, while golf packages, including green fees, are available from most of Edinburgh's top hotels (most of which are only half an hour away) or from hotels catering to golf enthusiasts in and around Gullane and North Berwick. For information on all the region's courses, green fees, club hire and accommodation packages, visit ⓦ www.golfeastlothian.com

Walking & cycling

It may not be easy to believe on a chilly winter's day with the wind biting off the North Sea, but East Lothian is the sunniest part of Scotland and great for walking. Hike up North Berwick Law or Traprain Law for great views across the border country and out to sea, or take a less energetic stroll along the John Muir Way from Musselburgh to Aberlady, or south from Dunbar. For cyclists (and

⬤ *Bass Rock*

drivers) there are three longer, waymarked trails from Musselburgh
to Dunbar – the 50 km (30 mile) Forth Coastal Trail, the 43 km
(27 mile) Hillfoots Trail through the foothills of the rolling
Lammermuirs, and the Saltire Trail through the heart of East Lothian.

Whisky tasting

The Glenkinchie distillery, at Pencaitland (25 km/16 miles) southeast
of Edinburgh, 3km/2 miles from Glenkinchie village) is one of the
few single-malt whisky makers in southern Scotland. Founded in
1837, it offers a tour of the stills and vats, a video presentation and –
best of all – a sampling of its finest products. Best not to take the
car, then. ● (01875) 342004 ● 09.00–17.00 May–Sept; 09.00–16.00
Mon–Fri Oct–Apr

Wildlife

For bird-watchers, the Lothian countryside and the Forth coast
are among the most exciting places in the British Isles, with
many migrant birds and huge colonies of seafowl. The Bass Rock
is the home of one of the world's largest gannet colonies, and
there are more accessible spots to see a range of waterfowl and
other birds at Levenhall Links, at the mouth of the River Esk near
Musselburgh, where tidal mudflats attract large numbers of
gulls, ducks, geese and waders, and hides and shallow pools
have been created to make viewing easy. A new Scottish
Birdwatching Resource Centre is being created at Aberlady
as the base of the Scottish Ornithologists Club and is planned
to open in 2006. Red deer and roe deer are sometimes seen in
the Lammermuirs, and other wildlife in the region includes
badgers, red squirrels, and otters – making a comeback on
waterways like the Esk and the Tyne.

For recommended companies offering wildlife-watching day trips and cruises on the Forth from Edinburgh and North Berwick, see the VisitScotland special wildlife site, Ⓦ www.wild-scotland.co.uk

TAKING A BREAK

The Lothian region has a wide choice of places to eat during the day and in the evening, ranging from basic pub food to lavish spreads in formal surroundings. Some of the best eating places include:

Bonar's ££–£££ This is an excellent spot for a special lunch or dinner, with an upscale restaurant and an informal brasserie. ⓐ Gifford Rd, Haddington ⓣ (01620) 822 100 ⓛ Wed–Sun only,

The Creel ££ This cosy restaurant near the old harbour serves excellent seafood. ⓐ Lamer St, Dunbar ⓣ (01368) 862 279

La Potiniere ££ This fine restaurant is under new ownership and is an ideal place for an extended lunch break, but reservations are essential at weekends. ⓐ Main St, Gullane ⓣ (01620) 843 214

The Waterside £–££ This riverside bar and restaurant has formal dining upstairs (reservations recommended) and a less stuffy bistro beside the river. It has a good choice of vegetarian offerings. ⓐ 1 Waterside, Haddington ⓣ (01620) 825 674

ACCOMMODATION

For help with finding somewhere to stay, contact the Edinburgh and Scotland Information Centre (see page 151)

The Borders

South of Edinburgh, within easy day-trip distance by bus or car, lies a patchwork of rich farming country dotted with small market towns and former mining villages, bordered by the rolling, grassy hills of the Southern Uplands – a region of moorland, sheep pastures, picturesque ruined abbeys, medieval castles and manor houses. Until the 18th century, the dales and hills of the border country were a debatable land, where local magnates took little notice of the royal powers of Edinburgh or London and where feuding and cattle raiding were a way of life, celebrated in the Border Ballads of Scotland's most famous author, Sir Walter Scott. Today, however, this is a far gentler landscape.

GETTING THERE

The main A7 and A68 roads connect Edinburgh with Melrose (about one hour) and Jedburgh (about 90 minutes) and points south. There are frequent buses (at least six per day) from Edinburgh's St Andrew Square Bus Station to Jedburgh, Melrose, Peebles and Galashiels. For bus and train timetables throughout Scotland, contact **Traveline** ☎ (0870) 608 2608 ⓦ www.traveline.org

TOURIST INFORMATION

Jedburgh Tourist Information Office ⓐ Murray's Green ☎ (0870) 608 0404 ⓛ open all year
Kelso Tourist Information Office ⓐ The Square ☎ (0870) 608 040 ⓛ open all year

Melrose Tourist Information Office ⓐ next to Melrose Abbey
ⓣ (0870) 608 040 ⓛ open all year
Borders Heritage ⓦ www.scottishborders.co.uk

SIGHTS & ATTRACTIONS

Jedburgh

Perilously close to the English border this picturesque country town, with its castle and medieval abbey, bore the brunt of many invasions from across the River Tweed. Its castle was destroyed by an English army in 1409, and its abbey, which was once one of the wealthiest religious foundations in Scotland, was sacked during Henry VIII's rough wooing of Scotland in 1544 (when Henry sought to bully the Scots into marrying the infant Queen Mary to his son) and was finally abandoned after the Protestant Reformation. Founded in the 12th century during the reign of the pious King David I (who also founded the Abbey of Holyrood in Edinburgh), the abbey ranks among Scotland's most picturesque ruins, with a tall stone tower, fine ornamental stone carvings, and a striking Catherine window in its gable wall. An excellent video show brings the abbey's turbulent history to life. Scotland's ill-fated queen is said to have stayed at the house now known as Mary, Queen of Scots House in 1566 and this attractive medieval building now houses a visitor centre which reveals her story. More recent is Jedburgh Castle Jail, a model prison built in 1824, with exhibits in the gloomy cells and in the former warden's home.

Jedforest Deer and Farm Park, south of Jedburgh, offers the chance to see herds of free-roaming red deer, raptors and an

Jedburgh Abbey

array of archaic breeds of sheep, cattle, pigs and barnyard fowl.

Jedburgh Abbey  Jedburgh 🕐 09.30–18.30 May–Sept; 09.30–16.30 Oct–Mar; admission charge

Jedburgh Castle Jail 🕐 10.00–16.30 Mon–Sat, 13.00–16.00 Sun; Jedburgh; admission charge

Jedforest Deer and Farm Park Camptown (8 km/5 miles south of Jedburgh on A68) 🕐 10.00–17.30 Easter–Aug; 11.00–16.30 Sept–Oct

Mary, Queen of Scots House Queen Street 🕐 11.00–16.45 Mon–Sat, 10.00–16.30 Sun, Easter–Oct; admission free

Kelso

Like so many of the border towns, Kelso is now a quiet little market town with little to show for its strategic importance in medieval times – except for the ruins of its abbey. West of Kelso, at Smailholm village, Smailholm Tower is a stern little relic of the Border wars – a four-sided 15th-century keep surrounded by an outer wall. Within is an exhibition of tapestries that once adorned the walls of local manors and a collection of dolls dressed as characters from Sir Walter Scott's famous Minstrelsy of the Scottish Borders. Floors Castle, just outside Kelso, is the ancestral seat of the local magnates, the Dukes of Roxburghe, and is grandly decorated and furnished with some superb antiques, and Mellerstain House, also nearby, is a fine Georgian stately home designed by William and Robert Adam, architects of parts of Edinburgh's New Town. The residence of the Earls of Hamilton, it too has splendid interiors.

Floors Castle Kelso 🕿 (01573) 223 333 🕐 10.00–16.30 Apr–Oct; admission charge

Mellerstain House Gordon, near Kelso 🕿 (01573) 410 225 🕐 12.30–17.00 Mon, Wed–Fri & Sun May–Sept; admission charge

Smailholm Tower 10 km (6 miles) west of Kelso on A6089/B6937

ⓘ (01573) 460365 ⓛ 09.30–18.30 May–Sept; 09.30–16.30 Oct–Apr; admission charge

Lauder

This small town's main attraction is the nearby Thirlestane Castle. Reckoned to be one of the best-preserved castles in Scotland, this red sandstone fortified manor is everything a romantic stronghold should be, with an array of turrets and battlements. Within, it has lovely decorated ceilings dating from the 17th century, working Victorian kitchens, and an exhibition of historic toys.

Thirlstane Castle ⓐ Lauder ⓘ (01578) 722430
ⓦ www.thirlestanecastle.co.uk ⓛ Opening hours vary, call or see website; admission charge

Melrose & Galashiels

Melrose, on the banks of the River Tweed, is one of the most striking towns in the Scottish Borders – and one of the oldest. Although the Romans never fully controlled this part of the British Isles, they did build a defensive rampart, Antonine's Wall, between Firth and Clyde in AD 142. Later, they withdrew to the more easily defended line of Hadrian's Wall, but maintained outposts in the region to the north, which they knew as Valentia. Melrose was one of these, and the remains of a legionary fort can be seen beside the Tweed at Newstead, about 2 km (1 mile) east of the town centre. The Romans called it Trimontium, after the three Eildon Hills which overlook Melrose. The circular ramparts of an even older pre-Roman Iron Age fort can be seen on the northernmost of Eildon's triple summits, and there are fine panoramic views from the tall central summit. There are equally fine views of the Eildon summits from Scott's View, at Bemersyde near Melrose, named after Sir Walter Scott.

Legend has it that the famous author loved this viewpoint so much that during his funeral the hearse carrying his coffin paused here to allow him a last posthumous glimpse of his beloved border country.

St Cuthbert's Way, part of a pilgrimage route that in medieval times connected Melrose with the great abbeys of Northumbria, passes between the two tallest peaks of Eildon, and Melrose's fine abbey, though much ruined, is the most evocative sight in town. It was built by Cistercian monks in 1136 and reconstructed in the 14th century. Like the other great religious foundations of the Borders, it suffered from the depredations of English armies and Scottish Protestant reformers, but parts of the graceful nave and choir and much more of its elegant masonry have survived. There's also an interesting museum, with displays of Roman finds from the nearby fort and other relics including a casket containing the heart of Robert the Bruce, recently exhumed from its last resting place in the abbey gardens. Dryburgh Abbey, which dates from about the same period (it was built in 1150) and stands about 8 km (5 miles) south of Melrose, has been much less fortunate, and lies mostly in picturesque ruins except for part of the main abbey church. Sir Walter Scott is buried in the abbey grounds, which stand on the banks of the Tweed and are overshadowed by tall cedars.

Melrose virtually merges with Galashiels, on the west side of the Tweed, although a drab industrial estate lies between the two town centres. Gala has a slightly more modern and industrial feel than its neighbour – a hub of the Borders woollen industry for almost five centuries, it has a number of spinning and weaving mills and factory outlet shops (see Retail Therapy page 138). Abbotsford

◀ *Smailholm Tower*

House, outside Galashiels, was the home of Sir Walter Scott, who had it built in 1822 and stocked it with a collection of memorabilia associated with heroes of his romances of the Lowlands, Highlands and the Border region, including Rob Roy MacGregor's claymore and a flintlock pistol belonging to Viscount Claverhouse of Dundee. Claverhouse was known to his Jacobite friends as Bonnie Dundee, but to his Covenanter enemies as Bloody Claverhouse, for his ruthless suppression of opponents of King James VII and II during the strife of the 1690s, remembered in England as the Glorious Revolution, but in Scotland as the Killing Time.

Abbotsford House ⓐ 5 km (3 miles) southeast of Galashiels on the A7 ⓛ 09.30–17.00 Mon–Sat Mar–Oct

Dryburgh Abbey ⓐ St Boswells, 13 km (8 miles) south of Melrose on B6356 ⓘ (01835) 822381 ⓛ 09.30–18.30 Mon–Sat Apr–Sept; 09.30–16.30, 14.00–16.30 Sun, Oct–Mar; admission charge

Melrose Abbey ⓐ outskirts of Melrose off A7 or A68 ⓘ (01896) 822562 ⓛ 09.30–18.30 May–Sept; 09.30–16.30 Oct–Apr; admission charge

Penicuik

This unassuming village was once the centre of the local lead-mining industry. Lead is a key component in making crystal glass and the region also became a centre for fine glass-making, which is celebrated at the Edinburgh Crystal Visitor Centre, where you can watch skilled artisans cutting and engraving fine pieces of glassware. The centre also contains an interesting museum focussing on glass-making over the years, along with an array of beautiful Edinburgh Crystal.

Edinburgh Crystal Visitor Centre ⓐ Eastfield, Penicuik ⓘ (01968) 675128 ⓦ www.edinburgh-crystal.org ⓛ 10.00–17.00 Mon–Sat, 11.00–17.00 Sun

Roslin Glen & Rosslyn Chapel

Rosslyn's amazing medieval chapel, founded in 1446 by Sir William Sinclair, last of the Princes of Orkney, is a remarkable medley of elaborate stone-carving that is surrounded by myths and mysticism. Every inch of masonry within is covered with fantastic symbols and complex decoration, and its history has given rise to dozens of theories involving the vanished Templar crusaders, the Holy Grail, and many more mysteries. The famous Apprentice Pillar is the most striking feature, but the chapel also contains many pagan symbols, including several Green Men. Most curious of all are carvings that appear to represent plants found only in the Americas made almost half a century before Christopher Columbus sailed to the New World. These are claimed to give credence to the legend that Sir William's ancestor, Prince Henry Sinclair, made a transatlantic voyage of discovery several centuries before Columbus. Nearby Roslin Glen Country Park, beside the North Esk, surrounds the chapel and offers some beautiful country walks through woodland and below steep sandstone cliffs, with the chance to see roe deer, woodpeckers, kestrels and many more birds and animals.

Rosslyn Chapel ➌ Roslin ℗ (0131) 440 2159 Ⓦ www.rosslynchapel.org.uk 🕐 10.00–17.00 Mon–Sat, noon–16.45 Sun; admission charge

Roslin Glen Country Park ➌ off B7003 between Roslin Village and Rosewell ℗ (01875) 821 990 🕐 08.00–20.00 summer, 08.00–17.00 winter

Selkirk

This quiet, old-fashioned town was, for many years, the home of the Borders weaving industry. Though this hard-wearing, stylish and quintessentially Scottish cloth is now more commonly associated

with the Isle of Harris, in the Outer Hebrides, it takes its name from the River Tweed, which flows through Selkirk. Sir Walter Scott was the local magistrate for some 30 years, and his 19th-century courtroom in Selkirk is now a museum with portraits of Scott, Robert Burns, and the Selkirk-born Mungo Park, famed for his exploration of West Africa during the 19th century. Nearby, at Innerleithen, Traquair House is an atmospheric 13th-century keep and mansion with its own brewery, making some of Scotland's finest ales. Philiphaugh, just south of Selkirk, was the scene of a famous defeat for the Royalist cause under the Earl of Montrose at the hands of Cromwell's Parliamentarian troops during the Civil Wars of the mid-17th century.

Sir Walter Scott's Courtroom ⓐ Market Place, Selkirk 🕐 10.00–16.00 Mon–Fri, 10.00–14.00 Sat, Apr–Sept; admission charge

Traquair House ⓐ Innerleithen, 2 km (1 mile) off the main A72 road ⓘ (01896) 830323 🕐 12.30–17.30 Apr–Oct; admission charge

RETAIL THERAPY

Edinburgh Crystal Visitor Centre Shop ⓐ Eastfield, Penicuik ⓘ (01968) 675128 ⓦ www.edinburgh-crystal.org 🕐 10.00–17.00 Mon–Sat, 11.00-17.00 Sun. Huge choice of top-quality glassware and factory seconds at bargain prices (see also page 136).

Traquair House Craft Shop ⓐ Innerleithen ⓘ (01896) 830323 🕐 Same hours as Traquair House (see above). Sells candles and attractive handmade pottery, and you can also pick up a few bottles of Traquair's famously strong ale.

○ *Ornate carving at Rosslyn Chapel*

TAKING A BREAK

King's Arms £ This old-fashioned former coaching inn has been feeding pub meals to locals and passers-buy since the 17th century. ⓐ High Street, Melrose ① (01896) 822 143

Monte Cassino £ Unpretentious, simple Italian eating place serving the usual array of pizza, pasta and salads. ⓐ Old Station Building, Melrose ① (01896) 820 082

Marmions Hotel Restaurant ££ Good value brasserie-style restaurant, long established but does not rest on its laurels. ⓐ Buccleuch St, Melrose ① (01896) 822 245 ⓛ Closed Sundays

⬤ River Tweed at Kelso

Queen's Bistro ££ Affordable but surprisingly sophisticated bistro serving contemporary and traditional Italian dishes. ❷ Bridge St, Kelso ❶ (01573) 228 899

Roxburghe Hotel Restaurant ££ This restaurant has few rivals in the region for fine dining and a sophisticated wine list. ❷ Kelso ❶ (01573) 450 331

ACCOMMODATION

For help with finding somewhere to stay, contact the Edinburgh and Scotland Information Centre (see page 151).

ACTIVITIES

Fishing

The River Tweed offers some of the best, most challenging – and most expensive – dry fly fishing in Scotland and the best beats on its banks are booked at premium prices several years in advance.

Riding

The British Horse Society (ⓦ www.bhsscotland.org.uk) offers four circular horse-riding trails in the Midlothian area and also offers overnight accommodation for horse and rider.

Rugby

The Borders region is Scotland's rugby heartland. During the rugby season there are matches almost every Saturday in almost every Border town and visitors are welcome. For fixtures, see the Scottish Rugby Union website (ⓦ www.scottishrugby.org)

Skiing

The Pentland Hills, within sight of Edinburgh, offer year-round skiing even when there is no snow, with one of Scotland's longest established dry ski slopes at Hillend, just outside the city.
❶ (0131) 445 4433

Walking

Walks in the Lothian and Borders area range from gentle countryside ambles to strenuous uphill hiking, many within the Pentland Hills Regional Park, less than 30 minutes from Edinburgh city centre. There is also good walking on the Eildon Hills, near Melrose, and countryside rangers lead a programme of guided walks in the Borders. St Cuthbert's Way, starting at Melrose, is a 100-km (64-mile) long-distance walking trail that stretches across the border all the way to the island of Lindisfarne, off the Northumbrian coast.

Pentland Hills Ranger Service ❷ Regional Park HQ, Boghall Farm, Biggar Road, Edinburgh ❶ (0131) 445 3383 Ⓦ www.pentlandhills.org
Scottish Borders Council Countryside Rangers Service UK ❶ (01835) 824000 Ⓦ www.scotborders.gov
Midlothian Access to the Countryside ❶ (0131) 561 5303

Whisky Tours & Tasting

Visit the Glenkinchie Distillery at Pencaitland, just outside Tranent where the Rate brothers opened their still-house in 1837 and where Edinburgh malt whisky is still made, for a tour of the working distillery and a chance to sample (in moderation) its distinctive product. ❶ (01875) 342 004

---

❿ *Edinburgh Information Centre on Princes Street*

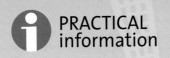

PRACTICAL
information

Directory

GETTING THERE

By air

Edinburgh International Airport is serviced by several daily scheduled flights from major British and European cities and there are some 40 flights a day from London to Edinburgh. Please note that UK residents still need to provide photographic ID to check-in with most airlines, usually a passport. Flight time from London is one hour. Low cost, no frills airlines such as easyJet and bmibaby also operate flights from the rest of Britain and Europe. Scotland's own no frills airline, flyglobespan, also has many flights between Edinburgh and Europe. There is a daily flight on Continental Airlines between Edinburgh and New York (flight time 7 hours and 40 minutes).

Edinburgh International Airport ⓦ www.edinburghairport.com

easyJet ⓦ www.easyjet.com

bmibaby ⓦ www.bmibaby.com

FlyGlobespan ⓦ www.flyglobespan.com

Continental Airlines ⓦ www.continental.com

By train

The GNER rail route from London King's Cross to Edinburgh Waverley passes through Peterborough, York, Doncaster and Newcastle. The journey time is approximately four hours.

GNER: ⓘ (08457) 48 49 50 ⓦ www.gner.co.uk

By coach

National Express coaches make the journey between London and Edinburgh eight times a day, with an average journey time of 11 hours, depending on traffic and time of day. Megabus is a budget

coach service that also links Edinburgh with London and
Manchester.

National Express ⓣ (08705) 808080 ⓦ www.nationalexpress.com
Megabus ⓣ (0901) 331 0031 ⓦ www.megabus.com

By car

Edinburgh is easily reached by the M1/A1 route and the M6/M74
motorways from the east and west of Britain respectively. Both the
AA and the RAC offer route planning services on their websites to
help plan your journey.

AA ⓦ www.theaa.com
RAC ⓦ www.rac.co.uk

ENTRY FORMALITIES

Documentation

A valid passport is the only documentation required for entry into
Great Britain for visitors from the Republic of Ireland, USA, Canada,
Australia, New Zealand, South Africa and members of the EU for a
stay of up to six months. Other visitors should consult the British
Embassy in their own country about visa requirements or check
with the website ⓦ www.ukvisas.gov.uk

Customs

There are almost no restrictions on what legal goods can be
imported or exported to and from other EU countries, as long
as you can prove that they are for your own use and not for
resale. Anything more than 3,000 cigarettes or 90 litres of wine,
for instance, would be considered suspicious and questions
will be asked. To import tobacco or alcohol you must be over the
age of 17.

For visitors from outside the EU, the restrictions on importing are as follows:

- 200 cigarettes **or** 100 cigarillos **or** 50 cigars **or** 250g of tobacco
- 60cc of perfume
- 2 litres of still table wine
- 250cc of eau de toilette
- 1 litre of spirits or strong liqueurs over 22 per cent volume **or** 2 litres of fortified wine, sparkling wine or other liqueurs
- £145 worth of all other goods including gifts and souvenirs.

MONEY

The pound (£) is the official currency of Great Britain. £1 = 100 pence. It comes in notes of £5, £10, £20, £50 and £100. Coins are in denominations of £1 and £2 and 1, 2, 5, 10, 20 and 50 pence. One aspect that often confuses visitors to Scotland is that Scottish banknotes come in three different designs, representing the Bank of Scotland, the Royal Bank of Scotland and the Clydesdale Bank. English banknotes are, however, entirely legal tender in Scotland. It might be advisable to change the notes back into English banknotes at the end of your stay. Even in England, where they are also legal tender, many smaller shopkeepers can be confused by them and refuse to take them, and they are extremely difficult to exchange abroad.

ATM machines (known as cashpoints) can be found outside banks and many other areas and are open 24 hours a day. The most widely accepted credit cards are VISA and Mastercard, but American Express is also accepted in larger hotels and more expensive restaurants and shops. Traveller's cheques and foreign money can be exchanged at larger banks and at bureaux de change.

HEALTH, SAFETY & CRIME

Visitors to Scotland are unlikely to encounter any food or drink issues – tap water is safe to drink although bottled water is also available everywhere.

Medical facilities are run by the National Health Service (NHS) which entitles British citizens and citizens of the EU to free medical care. Visitors from outside these areas should make sure they have adequate health insurance to avoid having to pay for any medical care should they fall ill. If you take prescriptive drugs, make sure you bring an adequate supply as well as a letter from your doctor or personal health record card. Most minor ailments can be diagnosed and treated at pharmacies throughout the city and, unlike many other countries, mild pain relief, such as aspirin, can often be bought at small grocery shops and in supermarkets, as well as at pharmacies.

Edinburgh has recently been voted the safest city in Europe, and visitors in the centre are unlikely to feel at risk in any way, although certain areas, such as the back streets of Leith, should be avoided at night. Any crime should be reported to the police straight away. Police officers can be seen regularly on the streets, dressed in black and white uniform and, often, fluorescent yellow jackets. They are friendly and efficient, and can be approached for anything from asking directions to reporting crime.

For advice on what to do in an emergency see pages 156–7.

OPENING HOURS

Shops 09.00–17.30 Mon–Sat. Some shops and department stores open later until 19.00 or 20.00 on Wednesday or Thursday, and have shorter opening hours on Sunday.

Banks 09.30–16.30 Mon–Fri. Some banks are also open on Saturday mornings. Cash can be obtained 24 hours a day from hole-in-the-wall ATMs.

Attractions opening hours for individual attractions are given next to their listing in the rest of the book.

TOILETS

Toilet facilities can be found in museums, department stores and shopping centres, and are generally clean and of a high standard. In pubs you would normally be expected to buy a drink before using the facilities, although many landlords and bar staff will kindly overlook this.

CHILDREN

Edinburgh is a child-friendly city and with the smoking ban in place even most pubs will be happy to have children on their premises, although it's always best to check first. All but the top

TELEPHONING EDINBURGH

Telephoning Edinburgh from abroad: dial 00 44 131 followed by the local number.

Telephoning abroad:

Australia: 00 61

Canada: 00 1

Republic of Ireland: 00 353

New Zealand: 00 64

South Africa: 00 27

USA: 00 1

National Operator Service: 100

International Operator Service: 155

restaurants will welcome children, and many offer children's menus. Breast-feeding in pubs and restaurants, however, is generally considered taboo.

Many attractions are specifically geared towards children, including Our Dynamic Earth (see page 70), the Museum of Childhood (see page 76) and the Edinburgh Dungeon on Market Street. Slightly older children will also get a lot out of the Royal Museum (see page 77) and the Museum of Scotland (see pages 76–7).

Baby food, nappies and other kiddie paraphernalia can be bought in supermarkets, in high-street chains such as Boots the Chemist and at grocery stores.

COMMUNICATION

Phone

The phone numbers given in this book are local numbers including the Edinburgh area code of 0131.

Public payphones accept either coins or credit cards. Some payphones also offer the option of texting messages. The minimum rate for a cash call is 30p; the minimum rate for a credit card call is 95p. Unlike much of the rest of the country, the classic red phone box can still be seen everywhere on Edinburgh's city streets.

Post

The British postal service is generally very reliable, with first-class mail arriving at destinations within the UK usually within one day, and in Europe within two or three days (depending on the service at the country of destination). The main post office in the city centre is in the St James's Centre (see page 96) which is open all day Monday to Saturday. Most other post offices in the city close at noon or 13.00 on Saturday. Stamps can be bought at post offices, as well as at larger newsagents. Postboxes on the street are the round, red pillar boxes, some of which have separate slots for national and international mail.

Current rates for sending postcards are: United Kingdom 30p (first class) or 21p (second class), Europe 42p, outside Europe 47p.

Internet

The easyEverything chain of internet cafés, established by the easyJet conglomerate, can be found at 137 Princes Street and 58 Rose Street in the New Town. Both are open seven days a week and offer great value at around £1 for an hour's worth of broadband access. Various other internet cafés, however, are dotted all over the city and you're never likely to be more than a few minutes away from web and email access.

ELECTRICITY

The standard electrical voltage in Britain is 240v with three square-pinned plugs. Foreign appliances will require an adaptor plug, available in your home country, and some US appliances running on 110v may require a transformer.

TRAVELLERS WITH DISABILITIES

Edinburgh is an old city, so cobbled and narrow streets as well as steep hills can prove a challenge for disabled travellers with mobility problems, especially in the Old Town. Many pubs too will prove difficult to access if you are in a wheelchair – even if you are able to enter the establishment, you may not be able to use the toilet facilities. Newer establishments, however, including museums, restaurants and bars, build disabled access into their design by law. Capability Scotland provides advice and information about disability issues, while Holiday Care is a national organisation that offers advice about holidays around Britain and transport issues for those with disabilities. Radar offers the same service, as well as advice for other countries.

Capability Scotland ⓐ 11 Ellersly Road, Edinburgh EH12 6HY ⓘ (0131) 313 5510 ⓦ www.capability-scotland.org.uk

Holiday Care ⓐ 7th Floor, Sunley House, 4 Bedford Park, Croydon CR0 2AP ⓘ (0845) 124 9971 ⓦ www.holidaycare.org.uk

RADAR ⓐ 12 City Forum, 250 City Road, London EC1V 8AF ⓘ (0207) 250 3222 ⓦ www.radar.org.uk

TOURIST INFORMATION
Tourist offices

The city's main tourist office is centrally located on Princes Street and stocks a range of leaflets, literature, guides and maps of the city and the surrounding area, as well as a small selection of souvenirs. Staff are knowledgeable and helpful and can offer advice on attractions, eating out, current events, accommodation, theatre tickets (including handling bookings), day trips and much more. There's also a very good information centre at Edinburgh Airport.

Edinburgh and Scotland Information Centre ⓐ 3 Princes Street ⓘ (0845) 22 55 121 ⓛ 09.00–18.00 Mon–Sat, 10.00–18.00 Sun, Apr & Oct; 09.00–19.00 Mon–Sat, 10.00–19.00 Sun, May, June & Sept; 09.00–20.00 Mon–Sat, 10.00–20.00 Sun, July & Aug; 09.00–17.00 Mon–Wed, 09.00–17.00 Thur–Sat, 10.00–17.00 Sun, Nov–Mar

Airport Information/Tourist Information Desk
Edinburgh International Airport ⓘ (0870) 040 0007 ⓛ 06.30–22.30 Apr–Oct; 07.00–21.00 Nov–Mar

The following websites also offer useful information:
- Ⓦ www.edinburgh.org
- Ⓦ www.visitscotland.com
- Ⓦ www.visitbritain.com

BACKGROUND READING
Non-fiction

Capital of the Mind: How Edinburgh Changed the World by James Buchan (John Murray, 2004). A history of the Scottish Enlightenment.

Edinburgh Curiosities by James U Thomson & Hamish Coghill (John Donald, 2005). A collection of fascinating stories of Edinburgh's people and events.

The Edinburgh Literary Companion by Andrew Lownie (Polygon, 2005). Traces the city's literary past and present.

One City (Polygon, 2005). A charity venture for the city, with perspectives on Edinburgh by natives Ian Rankin, Alexander McCall Smith and Irvine Welsh.

The Town Below the Ground: Edinburgh's Legendary Underground City by Jan-Andrew Henderson (Mainstream, 1999). A history of Edinburgh's tenements, such as that at The Real Mary King's Close (see page 50).

Weegies v Edinbuggers by Ian Black (Black and White, 2003). A humorous look at the rivalry between the two Scottish cities.

◀ *Lobster pots on Dunbar harbour*

Fiction

Boiling a Frog by Christopher Brookmyre (Abacus, 2002). Both thriller and satire set in the capital.

Complicity by Iain Banks (Abacus, 1994). Thriller set in various parts of the city including The Real Mary King's Close.

Fleshmarket Close by Ian Rankin (Orion, 2005). Just one of many of Rankin's thrillers following Inspector Rebus solving crimes in the city.

Heart of Midlothian by Sir Walter Scott (Oxford Paperbacks, 1999). Classic tale of 18th-century Edinburgh written in 1818.

The Prime of Miss Jean Brodie by Muriel Spark (Penguin, 1965). The classic Edinburgh novel set in the refined areas of Morningside and Comely Bank about a teacher and her female pupils as the *'crème de la crème'*.

Regeneration Trilogy by Pat Barker (Viking, 1996). Three novels brought together set in the Craiglockhart Hospital (now part of Napier University) during World War I.

Trainspotting by Irvine Welsh (Minerva, 1994). Modern classic of hard-hitting Leith and its drug-addled youths.

▶ *Traditional Edinburgh shopfronts*

Emergencies

EMERGENCY NUMBERS
In an emergency call:
Police ⓘ 999
Ambulance ⓘ 999
Fire Brigade ⓘ 999

Late-night Pharmacy ➋ 48 Shandwick Place ⓘ (0131) 225 6757
🕐 08.00–21.00 Mon–Sat, 10.00–17.00 Sun. You can find other late-night pharmacies by looking at the list on the door of any closed pharmacy.

🔺 *Melrose Abbey*